What others are saying about
How To Live With Your Self And Enjoy It

How to Live With Your Self and Enjoy It is a true treasure. Using an easy, conversational tone, and sharing stories from his own fascinating, yet highly relatable life, Dr. Don Hanley succeeds in creating a book that is deeply engaging, highly accessible, and—to use his own term—profoundly "life-giving." He skillfully weaves together an enchanting narrative of personal examples, choice words from other thinkers, and important relevant psychological and sociological tidbits. After reading this book, you will feel excited about the promise that your life holds, and inspired to co-create a world that is just, peaceful, and loving. I certainly was, and cannot wait to share this book with clients and friends!

GHADA OSMAN, PH.D., UNIVERSITY OF HARVARD GRADUATE, PRACTICING LMFT

In this book, Dr. Don Hanley not only imparts information but when the reader captures the spirit of what is written, a joyful transformation of his or her life can take place. This can lead, then, to a much deeper appreciation of one's life.

JOSEPH DILLON, PH.D, LMFT (RETIRED)

Many people feel their lives are "quietly desperate." Dr. Don Hanley offers an inspiration for all of us. His hope comes from his own remarkable life. His transparency inspires us to look honestly into ourselves and change for the better.

PATRICK PIROTTE, O.D. (OPTOMETRY)

What others are saying about
How To Live With Your Self And Enjoy It

After nearly a decade working in the pharmaceutical industry as a research scientist, I decided to pursue a career in the mental health field. I had the good fortune of meeting Dr. Don Hanley and having had the honor of being trained by him in the art of psychotherapy. Dr. Hanley is known for his compassion, wit, and his life-giving philosophies. This small book is a distillation of his philosophical ideas garnered over decades of therapy work and teaching psychotherapy to future counselors. I believe it is an essential guide for anyone who wishes to learn how to live with himself and enjoy it.

DR. EMILY CORNER, PH.D., M.A.

HOW to Live with YOURSELF and *Enjoy it*

Don Hanley, Ph.D.

A Word with You Press®
Publishers and Purveyors of Fine Stories in the Digital Age
Moscow, Idaho

ISBN: 978-0-9884646-9-8

How to Live with Yourself and Enjoy it
is published by:

A Word with You Press®

310 East A Street, Suite B, Moscow, Idaho 83843

For information, please direct emails to:
info@awordwithyoupress.com or visit our website:
www.awordwithyoupress.com

Cover design and interior layout: Teri Rider

First Edition, January 2016
Printed in the United States of America

10 9 8 7 6 5 4 3 2 1   16 17 18 19 20 21 22 23 24

FOREWORD

I am writing this small book with the hope that you will see your life's challenge as an evolutionary adventure that will help you develop into a person who enjoys life. Not because you have amassed a great fortune nor enjoy a luxurious life, but you have discovered who you truly are and are working to co-create a world that is more just, peaceful, and loving. You are doing this along with making a living, hopefully, doing what you enjoy. How you look at yourself and others is more important than what you are doing for a living.

I believe we are born to be lovers—not bedroom-kind but best-friend lovers—and even mystics far more than we are born to be warriors. If you are a Harry Potter fan, maybe we are born to be wizards rather than conforming non-thinkers.

This book asks you to explore life and ponder many ideas. It will not give you step-by-step guidance on how to live—which you wouldn't follow anyway even if I had the ability to write them. I present many ideas and theories that I have been pondering over my eighty-plus years of life. It is not a research treatise but a set of ideas and theories I have found helpful. I cite many people whose ideas inspired me. If you want to check them out or to see if I interpreted them correctly, please look them up. I am not interested in being right, but in inspiring you to ponder some ideas.

I have spent forty years supervising and mentoring counselors and psychotherapists and many former mentees have told me that they have kept a hyphenated word I often use—it is "life-giving," If I am asked whether or not doing this or that is good or bad, I will ask, "Is it life-giving?" I want to know if it enhances or hurts another person or persons' growth. If you steal anything from anyone, that is harmful to you and them; if you clean your parents' garage without being asked, that is life-giving. Even better, if you wake up in the morning and decide to have an enjoyable day, that is life-giving.

I believe that everyone on earth, regardless of their level of intellect, or athleticism, personality pleasantness, financial status, education, or any other measure, is gifted in some wonderful and positive ways. And because we were born human, we have the power to develop these gifts, or to allow these gifts to blossom forth. As the Star Wars films say, "May the force be with us."

This book is for anyone who is anxious or down about life or, simply, wishes to explore how a person might look at life. I like to think of the positive life being like a rosebud that is gradually opening up to become a beautiful blossoming rose. If you try to make it open, you will tear it apart—you have to nourish it and be patient as it gradually opens. You will change like the rose bud and just as the rose bud does not become a tulip, you will not become someone else—you will become your true self. I also believe that too many systems—including families, religions, schools, and work places—forget we are valuable and wonderful beings and treat us poorly.

I hope you enjoy reading this.

Don Hanley

TABLE OF CONTENTS

Chapter 1

FINDING OUR TRUE SELVES

I promise you that the discovery of your true self will feel like a thousand pounds have fallen from your back. You will no longer have to build, protect any idealized self image. Living in the True Self is quite simply a much happier existence.

Richard Rohr

THE ELUSIVE TRUE SELF

While working with people in various capacities for seventy years, constantly thinking about the meaning of life, and reading as much as I could in psychology, philosophy, theology, and the sciences, I believe that finding our *true* selves is a challenge of everyone's lifetime. So, when I entitled this booklet, *How to Live with Your Self and Enjoy It*, I saw it as a challenge of discovery.

And that challenge is a life-long adventure. Like the universe, finding our true self is beyond the thinking of our young self—it does take a long, thoughtful, and, hopefully, joyous time.

One day, a few years ago, I was thinking about atomic energy and marveling at the fact that a relatively small mass of atoms has enough potential energy to provide power for an entire population. Then I thought of my body that contains trillions of atoms. I, too, am packed with energy. What an interesting thought. And thought, itself, is fascinating. I somehow know that I am not just a physical body packed with energy and filled with atoms. What or who am I? I am different from rocks, plants, bugs, and animals. I am a human being, a person, a self. I am also part of a family, a tribe, or in our developing world, a nation. I see other beings somewhat like me—some are male, others are female, some are bigger, smaller, different colors, and speak different languages. What do I make of all this? How do I relate to these other beings? Unfortunately, most of us reached adulthood before we even began to explore the mystery of what it means to be a human being. I hope you will join me in that exploration now.

I, like one of the co-founders of humanistic psychology, Abraham Maslow, believe that a person is more than a more advanced animal. Maslow, after observing rats, pigeons, and other animals in his doctoral studies in psychology, held his first child and said, "This is more than a large white rat."

I believe that our life task is to evolve as beings who are able to discover, at least in part, who we are and to co-create a more just, healthy, life-giving, and loving world. I say, we evolve and as we do this, we formulate an exploratory self and gradually discover our *true* self. Some writers call this unrealized self, our *false* self. I prefer *exploratory* self as we are, hopefully, continually growing into our true self. I believe we intuitively already know our true self, but only obliquely—or in a cloudy sort of way. For instance, when we are born, we are one with our mothers. We are attached to her physically in the womb, and if all goes well, we continue to feel that attachment after our umbilical cord is cut. If for some reason, like our mother's disability or our own, we are separated from our mothers, our journey to discovering our true self has a more difficult task.

Ideally, naturally, and if we are fortunate, our mothers are healthy, cuddly, nurturing and see us as the most wonderful bundle of joy that ever existed. I did not see the birth of our first daughter but I did see the arrival of our second. I had been doing my best to coach my wife's efforts to relax and breathe and dry her forehead as she sweated through labor. Her face was contorted in anguishing pain and then the baby girl appeared and instantly, her face changed to a relaxed expression of pure joy. It is one of the most wonderful sights in the world. This most marvelous of creatures came into this world to begin discovering who she is.

We come into this world and we have had good experiences already—if we have come from a "good womb." We could also arrive with bad experiences, if our mother had an illness or traumatic pregnancy. In any event, we are here in the world and our challenge is to discover who we are. Because of our evident helplessness, we are taken care of by big people who are supposed to know what is best for us. The vast majority want the best for us, but a sizable proportion of them are not well-educated themselves in taking care of this new arrival. Let's take a little detour and find out how you were treated when you first came into this world. Our script on how to be in this world begins on day one. So let's explore this idea of script.

EXPLORING THE SCRIPT WE GREW UP WITH

I believe every person's life is worth at least one novel or play, or several novels and plays. Shakespeare said, "The world is a stage and all the men and women merely players." If you have ever been in a school play, you know that every person in the cast is given a copy of the script. If you were one of the main characters, you had to memorize many lines and learn the best way to perform many different actions. In our own lives, whether we realize it or not, we are the main character in our personal play and have created a script over several years. All of us have been told how to act, how to be believe and we have reacted to these messages and our reactions become our script. Some parts of our script are good and some negative and create problems that we must work to overcome. If you were born with exceptionally good intelligence and were encouraged and coached to use that gift well, it became a positive part of your script. If you were told that you are stupid, even if you had that good intellect, then you might doubt yourself and work harder to discover your gift. I encourage you to look over your script and evaluate it—see what you want to keep and what you would like to discard. I will share with you a part of my own script and hope you will do the same with yours.

I, like you and everyone else, learned about my birth from others. In my case, it was from my sister who was twenty-two years older than me, and who was in attendance at my birth.

It was three o'clock in the morning and my mother had been quite weak as she had recently survived having diphtheria, the death of my infant brother and eight-year-old sister to diphtheria. Mom weighed less than one hundred pounds. I was the ninth child and sixth boy. The birth did not go well as Mom continued to bleed profusely and the doctor and the nurses had to work for hours to keep her from dying.

Of course, I was not a bundle of joy for my parents and siblings. My dad and siblings, other than my sister, had already left Nebraska for Kansas, where Dad was going to try tenant farming.

I came into this world, like all babies, as needy—but a little more so because of circumstances.

I did not realize the consequences for many years but that bleak beginning was not helpful—and it wasn't anyone's fault. Because I was "just another mouth to feed," I believed that I wasn't lovable, nor wanted. I felt like an abandoned orphan for years.

LIFE IS WORTH LIVING REGARDLESS OF THE BEGINNING

I believe everyone's life is worth living, so I encourage you not to say, "Well, my life isn't worth looking at." Or, "My life sucks and I don't want to look at it. I just want to start over." Our lives define who we are and if we wish to enjoy it, we need to own it, and develop it with as much authenticity as possible. People like Helen Keller, who was blind and deaf yet became a world renowned writer and speaker. Look at *The Miracle Worker*, a film about Helen Keller's early life when she was a "wild child." Or think of Nelson Mandela, who spent twenty-seven years in a prison doing hard labor, and yet emerged as a loving and enlightened statesman. Obviously, they did not follow the negative parts of the scripts that they had earlier formulated. More recently, Amy van Dyken, who was an Olympic gold-medalist in 1996 and 2000, and in 2014 was in an accident that paralyzed her from the waist down. A reporter accompanied her on a shopping trip. Amy was unable to reach something on a shelf and laughed, saying, "Isn't this fun?" The reported said, "You just said 'fun?'" Amy responded. "I need to have fun learning how to live fully as a paraplegic." The reporter then said, "I saw you when you won the gold. You were fabulous!" Amy responded, "I'm still fabulous, but now I'm a paraplegic." Amy managed to establish a script that read, "I am more than my physical ability, I am a marvelous being."

I edited much of my script, but unconsciously kept some of it—some good and some bad—as does everyone. I was born in March, 1933, the worst year of the Great Depression. The spirit of depression seeped into the very bones of everyone in my family. It seemed as if the infinite energy that we all inherit had vanished from the world. If, when I was six years old and started school and was able to read, my script would have said, "You are dressed in ill-fitting, hand-me-down clothes, and look sad, as if you'd never experienced joy. You walk with your head down and slightly bent over like an old man. You seem afraid of anyone bigger than you and of anything new." So, my script definitely needed editing.

For better and for worse, our family members help us write our scripts and the best we can do is put as positive a spin on their words and actions as we can. Ideally, parents and older siblings are good gardeners who nourish us and help us to grow. I have found that we are lucky if we have one or two good "gardeners"—a nurturing grandparent or other relative. It seems that all of my family members were merely survivors who could hardly nourish themselves, let alone do more for the younger kids than help find food and shelter.

Dr. Abraham Maslow, author of *Motivation and Personality*, is famous for his hierarchy of needs. Unlike Freud and others, he believed we humans are primarily motivated by our needs, rather than by our inner drives or conditioning. He says that first, we need to survive—to satisfy our basic physical needs—food, clothing and shelter. "For a starving person, paradise is a place with food." My parents went to heroic lengths to provide our basic needs. They also did their best to provide the following needs: safety and security, followed by love and belonging, and self-esteem. Of course, I, like all young children, could not understand that often our care-givers were too worn out and sick to provide attention and the kind of loving kindnesses that all children need. In my family, eight of the children survived, so, in a way, they did well just to see that we were fed and sheltered. Unfortunately, the majority of families in the world are still barely surviving.

Back to my script: I started the first grade believing I was stupid, clumsy, ugly, and quite worthless. For some reason, I had a bladder problem and often wet my pants before morning recess and was sent home. One school morning, my dad was home when I arrived. He took one look at me and my wet pants, back-handed me, knocked me to the floor, and yelled, "You're nothing but a worthless little piece of shit." Of course that was not true, but at the time it defined me. It was years later that I learned that dad was going through his own set of troubles, but that did not help my six-year-old self. After teaching and counseling many men and boys, I know that some heard similar things from parents and ignored them. I, like many others, absorbed it and let it hurt me. Religion was not helpful and even made it worse.

I was born into the Catholic faith and in the spring of the first grade, at age seven, I was required to make my first confession and first Communion. The first confession was a horrible experience. I confessed that I and some other kids played naked and touched each other "down there." The priest told me, in a very condemning tone of voice, that I had committed a mortal sin that could send me to hell. I knew about hell. It was a place where I would burn up over and over again forever. So I left the confessional crying and looked up at the frightful twenty foot high mural above the altar. It depicted an angry

God the Father. I said my penance knowing that I was not only a stupid little shit but I was also hated by God because I was a terrible sinner. When I made my first Communion on the following Sunday, I thought the song we sang before Communion, *Oh Lord, I am not worthy,* definitely applied to me.

That year, and the "brand" of being a sinful worthless shit, was burned into my evolving little brain and I was a long ways away from thinking I was gifted in any way—or in any way close to discovering my real self. My only consolation in those early years was having time with our collie-shepherd dog, Pal, who waited for me every day about three blocks from home. He was there no matter what time of day I was sent home from school. I often wished that he could talk. I know he would have said I was a good guy. Can a dog be a small boy's savior? I did my best not to disturb anyone for anything for the next four years. I believe it was a way of feeling "safe." So I wrote in my script: be quiet and unimportant. My script was, unhappily, not unique—many of us started life in self-esteem debt.

If you are a teacher, minister, parent, grandparent or any kind of helping professional, please remember what you were like when you were a child and how easily you were influenced by the "big people" who knew so much about everything—or so you thought. Be a good gardener who nurtures the growth of your charges and not a carpenter who pounds it into place. Far too often, I have encountered persons of all ages who were told, in some way, that they are worthless. If you were one of them, do your very best to turn down the volume of that message. You cannot erase it completely, but you can turn it into a memory rather than a haunt of a perceived "truth."

The script of my first ten years of my life, stated that I was a miserable little person whom no one liked or cared about. I did my best to hide from everyone. I longed for someone to tell me that I was okay, or wanted, or was worthwhile in some way. If I saw a movie where an adult hugged a child or kissed him, I cried. I wondered if such fairy-tales ever came true. It surely wasn't in my script.

When I was teaching a religious education class for teachers in the 1960s, I ran across an article entitled *A Cipher in the Snow*. ("Cipher" is a little used word. It means a person of no consequence, a non-entity.) It was a true story written by a teacher who had been asked to write an article about a boy in his class who had died on his way home on the school's bus. Because he didn't really know the boy because he was so quiet, the teacher interviewed the bus driver, who reported, "He was a very quiet boy and never caused any trouble at all. That day, he just slowly walked up the aisle of the bus, tapped me on the shoulder and whispered, 'Please stop the bus, I need to get off.' So at the next stopping place I stopped and he got off the bus and kind of staggered about three steps and fell in the snow. I got off the bus and knelt down. He wasn't moving at all. I said, 'What's the matter, son?' He didn't respond. I felt his pulse and there just wasn't any. I went up to the nearest house and asked a nice lady if I could use the phone and called for an ambulance." The bus driver had tears in his eyes as he said, "That was so sad." The teacher went to the boy's home and met his very depressed mother and a drunk step-father and neither one seemed to care about the boy's death. Only the mother and a couple of dozen students attended the funeral. The teacher wrote, "From that day on, I was never going to let another child in my class become a cipher."

My childhood had some sadness, but nothing like what must have happened to the boy in that article. I cried every time I read the article as did the teachers in my classes when I read the article aloud.

In my early years, I probably would not have been moved by a beautiful old myth about God. That myth has God's angels getting more and more worried about humans who seem to be getting smarter all of the time. They worried that maybe someday humans might learn what marvelous creatures they are and de-throne them. So the angels began to plot where they could hide the truth about how wonderful humans are. One angel says, "Let's hide the truth on the highest mountain." Another responds, "No, they will climb to it." A third angel says, "Let's hide it in the deepest part of the ocean." A response was, "No, they'll swim to it." They went back and forth for days and finally, one angel said, "I know where we'll hide the truth from man! We'll hide it in his heart—then he will doubt it!"

I don't think it is the angels who hide the truth from young children—it is the many negative people around them.

I hope you, the person reading this, were fortunate enough to have most of the people who were positive and thought you were a "great big bundle of joy," as one song puts it. Don't take it for granted and do pass it on to your children and all children you encounter.

Wonderful gifts can be found in the heart of people who are in the strangest, and even most difficult of circumstances. One of the most influential professors in my graduate studies was Dr. Victor Frankl who survived three years in Auschwitz concentration camp. He tells us in his book, *Man's Search For Meaning*, that every morning he told himself that there was one thing that he had that no one could take away from him and that was his *ability to decide* his own *attitude* every day. And he decided, in the midst of winter in frozen Poland, with little food and no coat, to have a good day. To continue that day after day without knowing how or when things were going to end, is one of the most amazing things I've ever heard of. Another thing Frankl did that helped him to survive was to *visualize* his wife—see a picture of her in his mind and heart. She had been in another section of the camp and had been killed, but Victor did not know that while he was imprisoned. I wished he had shared with us what his childhood was like and whether or not this positive outlook on life helped him develop this positive script. I was happy to put it in my script when I was in my thirties. It would have been wonderful if I could have put it there when I was a child.

There are more people who, like Victor Frankl, found ways of making their lives flourish. One is a kind and loving friend who also survived Auschwitz, Yaja Boren. She could easily be a bitter woman, but she is not. She, too, has written of her experience, in a wonderful book entitled, *We Only Have Each Other*. When asked her religious affiliation, she responds, "Loving Kindness." And she lives it. Her autobiography states that her family, although extremely poor, were very kind and loving. She felt loved and cherished. I asked her if this helped her and her sister survive. She replied, "Oh, of course."

Today, I believe many of us have come up with a script that believes that possessions, social status, financial or political power, physical beauty and strength, will make us feel worthy. If we have kept that script, it is because we fail to look into our own hearts—and the values imparted to us in our scripts. So our task is to find our own hearts—and our healthy scripts—by exploring our habits and beliefs. We must discover what was pounded into our dear little heads and if it was not positive and encouraged us to feel our giftedness, find our bliss, and our ability to easily connect to others—then we must work to change what needs changing.

A positive and true self will not be found in owning the 'best' or most expensive *anything*. But, seeing all the storage units in our country now, there are lots of people trying to find *it* in "stuff." I wonder if some of them think they may have accidentally packed happiness, and a positive script, away in one of the storage units. Ah, the great bumper sticker: "He who dies with the most stuff wins."

Dr. Maslow stated that after our physical and safety and security needs are met, we need love and belonging, and then, self –esteem. I believe that too many Americans seek self-esteem in the above mentioned financial and social status rather than in finding love and belonging in our living. Becoming a loving person, as we know, is not easy, and constantly nurturing that love is a life-long process. Usually, we need to change, or at least adjust, our inherited script. I began to find a flicker of hope when I was eleven years old.

I will share some choices and script changes I began to make in the next chapter.

Chapter 2

CHOOSING TO CHANGE OUR SCRIPTS

A problem cannot be solved using the same consciousness that caused the problem in the first place.

Albert Einstein

Sometimes the points of view of the optimist and the pessimist are placed before me so skillfully balanced that only by sheer force of spirit can I keep my hold upon a practical, livable philosophy of life. But I use my will, choose life and reject its opposite—nothingness.

Helen Keller,
The Open Door

If we want to change the script we grew up with, we must choose, as Helen Keller said, "by sheer force of spirit" to make the change and to choose a more life-giving path. We have no control over the handicaps, or short-comings, or even the seminal giftedness we were born with, but we can choose life, just as Helen Keller did; she was both blind and deaf, but she chose life. We could say that she was scripted to be a handicapped invalid and perhaps, spend her life in an institution or at least be a burden on her family. But she decided to change her script and to choose life. And what a wonderful life she chose, becoming a world renowned inspirational author and speaker. I hope that you, like me, tell yourself often that if she could live a positive life with her handicap, then I can also.

Dr. Alice Miller, a Swiss psychiatrist, researching Adolph Hitler's life, wrote, in her book *For Your Own Good*, that, before he was born, his mother had lost three babies in their early infancy. She feared that she had given them too much care and decided to give little or no care to baby Adolph. Miller also learned that his father physically punished him nearly every day. So Adolph grew up as a maternally abandoned and severely abused child. We could say that he was scripted to be bitter and hateful and, although he was gifted in many ways, he did become a hateful and life-destroying person and, many say, one of the most monstrously evil persons who ever lived. Does his violent family upbringing excuse him from the destruction of life that he inflicted on millions of people? I certainly believe that it does not—he chose a life-destroying script, not a life-giving one.

Many people have had horrible childhoods but ended up choosing to be wonderfully loving and creative people. So, my firm belief is that there are many things we cannot change but there are some very important things we can change. Hopefully, we chose a lovingly creative script and to behave in a way that is life-giving to ourselves and to others. We are free to choose a hurtful and destructive script but can *choose* otherwise.

In recent years, researchers in child development have learned that the infant in the womb has consciousness and begins to form beliefs about life. If that infant finds himself in a "good womb", that is a consistently serene place in which the mother has good health, drug and alcohol free, no physical or emotional abuse, then that infant comes into the world feeling serene and positive. If she begins life in a "bad womb" that is awash in alcohol, drugs, emotional and physical abuse or stress, then she is born in distress. Naturally, the "good womb" baby is a more delightful little person to be taken care of and the latter, a difficult one—through no fault of his or her own.

Researchers also state that the first "core belief" a child develops is whether or not the world is *safe*. If the infant has his or her physical and emotional needs met regularly, then the world is safe for them. If the baby is neglected, hurt, or if the environment is chaotic then he or she does not feel safe. This infant, even before turning one year old, believes the world is dangerous, then it must be constantly vigilant and defend itself in some way.

As I'm sure you know, we do not all get started in life having come from a "good womb," a wonderfully nurturing crib life, and warm and stable mother and other care-givers. We all begin life in a continuum of very toxic and horrible to warm and wonderful. As you are aware from chapter one, my mother's womb was not a good place, through no fault of her own. Often it is helpful if we can learn the circumstances of our mother's pregnancy and early care so we have a clearer idea of why we seem to have more difficult challenges then some other people.

I have also known many people who were born with the proverbial "silver spoon" in their mouths—both emotionally and physically—but grow up to be vain, selfish, and negative people no one wants to be around. The "silver spoon" may come with a script that the child is superior to other humans and thus they learn only disdain and power-over other people. They, like all of us, need to choose to include in their script love and creativity. We choose what kind of person we wish to be, regardless of our beginnings. We have the challenge of becoming the wonder-filled persons who will have a happy life, or a person who squanders their gifts and become hurt-giving people.

I believe I developed a negative attitude toward "silver-spoon" people when I was in the first grade. We were quite poor and one day I was sitting on a bench near the school playground and putting a new piece of cardboard in my shoe to cover the hole. A sort-of cousin-in-law third grader stopped by and looked down at me. She had a fur-collared coat and muff to keep her hands warm. She sneered at me and said, "You are such an embarrassment. You are just white trash." Feeling hurt, I later asked my mother if we were white trash and she responded, "We are poor now, but we are not trash. Whoever said that was talking trash." It helped a little but I kept the memory.

On Chosing To Develop Our Own Scripts

Choosing to be life-giving is also to choose happiness. Modern positive psychology says that our happiness involves *pleasure, engagement, and meaning,*' and is characterized by feelings of joy, gratitude, serenity, interest, hope, pride, and amusement (Shawn Achor's *The Happiness Advantage*). If you were among those who began life in a "good womb" and had early positive nurturing, you probably have experienced these emotions in abundance.

If we wish to be positive life-givers, we must choose these characteristics, even if we really don't know, from experience, what these emotions are. Our negative script may have come from growing up in an alcoholic family, or had mentally ill parents, and had suffered physical abuse, homelessness, racial prejudice, extreme poverty, and the list can go on and on. Often, as children, parents, teachers, and other care-givers had already scripted a person as severely as people in prison camps. It takes a long time to overcome a molestation, rape, or parents calling you horrible, negative names. After working with many adults who have survived extremely difficult experiences in their lives and who still wish to be creatively happy in their mid and late years, I think they should receive some kind of civilian Purple Heart.

Too often, our families and schooling do not encourage us to choose what kind of script we wish to have. Care-givers, teachers, and other adults believe they always know what it best for us. We are told when to get up in the morning, what to wear, what to eat, who to play with, what television programs to watch, when to go to bed, and on and on. We are forced to be just like every other "good" child. Even, if asked, no one knows where to find these so-called good children. Often fear impels parents to become "helicopter parents" who know exactly what their children are doing every minute of the day—and think they are doing good when they try to micro-manage every move their child makes. We are born free and, as Jean Paul Sartre says, "We are condemned to be free." So the micro-managing parent only breeds resentment in the child.

I believe, and statistics demonstrate, that the world now is no more dangerous than it was decades ago when I grew up. The big difference is that now we have television, computers, and radios telling us all, 24/7, of the disasters and dangers in our world. We are *supposed* to feel afraid, it seems, and so parents, with good intentions believe they are protecting their child from unknown dangers.

ON LEARNING TO CHOOSE

Despite the negative things I experienced in my early years, I did have quite a bit of freedom until I was eleven years old. I chose my own companions outside the family and put shoes on only when it was cold or for school and church. As mentioned earlier, I began school when I was six years old and in the first grade. Even though my mom often said, "I don't know what I'm going to do with you," and Dad condemned me as stupid and worthless, I did have and kept the gift of freedom. The worst outcome was that I was sure everyone saw me as worthless no matter how hard I tried to be "nice."

Because of his grand-mal seizures, my dad was sent to a Kansas state mental hospital. Mom and the four youngest moved to California when I was eight. I stayed hidden as best I could for three years. I wasn't so much angry and bitter, as fearful. When I was eleven, Dad had been released from the hospital and got a job managing a small lumber yard in Edgemont, South Dakota. He asked that Mom and the four youngest children join him there. Of course, we did not have a choice. Mom was barely making it financially, so she had no choice either. Our beginnings in a new state did not begin well. Dad expected all six of us to live in a 12 by 20 foot bungalow attached to the lumber yard.

Mom objected and rented part of an old house for $25 a month. They argued for several days and then, one day, while I was raking up leaves in the back yard of the old house, I heard Mom scream. I ran into the house and Dad was hitting her. I grabbed his arm, he backhanded me and knocked me down. I ran to the police station a block away. The policeman and I went back to the house. Dad was standing in the front yard and he and the policeman talked. I went into the house, Mom was crying and I decided that I would never be angry like Dad. It was a promise that I kept for many years—but broke when I had a family of my own. Mom left Edgemont and stayed with our oldest sister in Kansas for ten months.

During that year, Dad asked me to help him at the lumber yard. I felt needed and wanted for the first time in my life. I guessed Dad was kind of like me—sometimes good and sometimes bad. Another good fortune came my way when Father Groel, a kindly old priest, walked across town to ask me to serve daily Mass for him. Even better, Ms. Reed, a large spinster lady who loved children, was my fifth-grade teacher—and, miracle of miracles, she thought I was smart. During that fifth-grade year, I began to feel even more worthwhile when Dad fell and broke his leg. He had to be in the hospital miles away—and I got to run the lumber yard for an entire week. I served Mass at 6:30 in the morning, opened the yard at 8:00, made out sales tickets, made the bank deposits, and daily reports to the main office. I no longer was a miserable, worthless piece of shit. I was important and could do important things.

I hope you can recall times in your early life when you made some important changes in your outlook on life—and thus changed part of your script.

When Mom returned from Kansas the following June, she and Dad fought again and they divorced. My two sisters, being afraid of Dad, chose to live with Mom. I received the best gift of my life—the freedom to choose who I wanted to live with. I thought life would be easier if

I lived with Mom, but I would learn more and be important if I lived with Dad. I chose Dad and lived with him until he died three years later. I firmly believe that a child should be given as many choices as he or she is capable of making and when ten or older, he or she should be given increasingly important life choices. When possible and necessary, if there is a divorce, choose which parent he or she wants to live with.

BE RESPONISBLE AND MAKE AS MANY CHOICES AS POSSIBLE

I would like to say that I began to make positive choices all by myself but, honestly, my three adult "educators"—Dad, Father Groel, and Ms. Reed—allowed me to break the cycle of thinking I was worthless and stupid. Too often our education adds to the abuse by parents, other adults, and teachers telling us that we don't know anything and don't have brains enough to make good decisions about nearly anything. "You just shut up, sit still, and I'll tell you what to read, say and think." This disabling attitude toward children and education was encouraged by the theory that we are born with a mind that is a *tabula rasa*—a blank slate—that needs to be written on. Dr. Alice Miller tells us that there is a long history of parents believing that children must be forced to be human. She cites many examples from earlier texts on parenting. Here are two:

> *If your son does not want to learn because it is your will, if he cries with the intent of defying you, if he does harm in order to offend you, in short, if he insists on having his way: Then whip him well till he cries so: "Oh, no, Papa, oh no!" Such disobedience amounts to a declaration of war against you.*

> —Krager, *Thoughts on the Education and Instruction of children*, 1752

I have never yet found willfulness in an intellectually advanced or exceptionally gifted child...Willfulness must be broken at an early age by making the child feel the adult's unquestionable superiority. Later on, shaming the child has a more lasting effect, especially on vigorous natures for whom willfulness is often allied with boldness and energy.

—Grunwald, 1899, *On the Character Faults of Willfulness in Children.*

I hope that you, like me, are rather horrified at the above ideas, and at the same time notice some familiarity—if not to your own life, then in others. I believe that many people too often feel inadequate or too tired to take on the challenges of making choices, and so they turn to someone or some organization to tell them what to do and how to live. I still get chills when I see old newsreels of Nazi Germany showing thousands of people saluting and shouting, "Heil Hitler."

Some religions state that if we want to be happy and go to heaven then we must be perfect—and being perfect means following all of the rules that particular religion dictates. Often, when we are young, it seems important, if we are to survive, to choose to follow the prescriptions given by our parents and their chosen teachers and care-givers. At the same time, it is important to begin to evaluate what we think is life-giving and positive and what is not. Too often a teenager, after having ideas too forcefully fed to him or her, rejects everything and chooses a negative lifestyle, or the opposite, gives up any desire to choose and blindly follows the dictates of her elders, or seeks other "masters" to follow—like gang leaders. Of course, I believe we should evaluate everything and choosing what we believe is best after careful evaluation.

When I was twelve, I made another decision that proved helpful later in life. In January of my sixth grade I saw the film, *The Keys of the Kingdom*, about a missionary priest to China. Gregory Peck played the priest who was courageous, compassionate, intelligent, good, and a talented builder. I wanted to be like that and, at the end of the movie, I left the little movie theatre, looked up at the snowy sky, and whispered aloud, "God, I'm going to be a priest." I knew I could build a church, a school, convent and other buildings. My big fear was that I wasn't smart enough or good enough.

I began studying extra hard so I could be smart. In order to work on being good, I decided to end my evening prayers by counting all the good and positive things I did that day—completed homework as best I could, went to Mass, obeyed the teacher, chopped wood, swept the floor, did the dishes, straightened two lumber piles, made my bed, complimented Dad on his cooking (even when it wasn't very good). I had to be able to count ten things I had done that day or I felt shame and guilt. When Dad died when I was fourteen, I gave up the counting but still worked to become a perfectionist pain-in-the-ass. That was a part of my self-created script that I had to work hard to erase later in life.

CONTINUING TO DISCOVER WHO WE ARE

The first half of life is the time to find out who we are. It is the time to look at our script and develop our *exploratory self*. During that period, hopefully, we will experiment making choices that will make up our wonder-filled self. I like a theory of an inspirational professor, Dr. Bernard Boelen, who thought every person who made it past forty, or, sometimes, fifty or more, had three adolescences. The first is from infancy to childhood (the 'explosive twos and threes'); the second, from childhood to adulthood, is from thirteen to twenty five (what we usually think of as adolescence) and the third adolescence, from adulthood to true maturity, coming between thirty-five and fifty. Dr..

Boelen stated that the early adult years, from the mid twenties to forties, is the time for practical living—choosing a profession, getting and keeping a job, buying a house, raising children, and all. I was in my early thirties and a priest when I heard this theory and I was already getting very uncomfortable in my role as a priest, so the next step toward true maturity was a welcome idea.

The third adolescence is the full blossoming into true maturity or being our *true* self– if we continued to make positive choices during our exploratory self-time— from infancy through early adulthood. If we continued to choose to grow in various ways, by the time we make it through the third adolescence, we will be flourishingly human, as Aristotle called happy  persons, and we grow into our true selves. My professor was convinced that only a minority go through this "crisis of the limits" (third adolescence) successfully and emerge as truly mature people. Most, he contended, stay stuck and continue using all their energy making more money, getting bigger houses and more expensive cars. Too often they are looking for fulfillment *only* in obtaining more material things and gaining some kind of social status, or power over others. Of course, there are those who are even worse and never seem to go anywhere other than a life of addiction and/or crime. I have known several men and women who did not make truly life-giving choices until they were in their forties and fifties, and then began to blossom into wonderfully creative and mature people.

A wonderful spiritual writer, Thomas Merton, would agree with Dr. Boelen but called the exploratory adult self, the "false self." That is, he or she is being the person who is tied to his early conditioning and survival needs or desire to succeed in a way that will impress others. Merton would say that the true self is free to just be him or herself. When I first heard these ideas in I was in my thirties, I thought I was beginning to find my true self. Perhaps I was making a beginning but that was all. I have been evolving ever since and I think, after fifty years, I still have a way to go.

Seeking Help As We Continue To Grow

If you think you are still not free from feeling worthless and are living a miserable life, and are what shrinks call depressed and/or anxious, you can seek help from some wise or, unfortunately, sometimes not-so-wise people. If you are fortunate, you have one friend who is a true confident and will share with you his or her thoughts and feelings—in a warm, loving, and blameless way. And equally fortunate, you are such a friend like that to other people. Too often, some of those we call "friends" just want to give bad advice and be bossy. In any case, do feel free to examine your feelings and thoughts and choose your path—and take responsibility for the path you take.

If having supportive friends and family is not possible or not enough, I hope you are not too proud to seek out a counselor or psychotherapist. Do keep in mind that a traumatic infancy and childhood is often the cause of adult difficulties and effective therapy can be very helpful. A person sometimes needs to see two or more therapists before finding one with whom he or she really connects—someone who is warm, authentic, compassionate and professional in every way. It is important that we feel this person is one we feel safe and comfortable with, even if we might need to travel many miles to find the right person.

It is possible that we need medicine to help us, especially if we are severely anxious, have a deep depression, are delusional and out-of-touch with ordinary reality, or are bi-polar. If the depression or anxiety is severe, medication can lift the symptoms and will help therapy work. A psychiatrist will sometimes recommend a psychotherapist who will help you get in touch with your core beliefs and help you discover your strengths and realize how wonder-filled you really are. She will also help you become responsible for changing your negative thoughts and behaviors. Medicine, without therapy, too often just glosses over our miserable feelings, and like some ineffective therapist's efforts, we walk around looking quite calm and happy, but remain the same miserable person inside.

Too many behavioral psychologists believe we are simply very complex conditioned animals—like rats and monkeys, only larger and more complex. Sigmund Freud insisted that we were blindly motivated by innate drives for the necessities of life: water, air, food, sex and power. I believe that we do have these drives. Also, I believe Maslow's research on "self-actualizing people"—that is, on people who seemed to be living full and happy lives, is more important. Again, it is not either-or, but both-and. Thinkers like Maslow, Carl Rogers (book: *On Becoming a Person*), and other "humanistic" psychologists, as well as most religious thinkers believe that, yes, we are conditioned but we are *free* to choose how we will live and satisfy those needs. I've mentioned two basic needs—physical needs and safety and security. And last of the dependency needs—the needs that depend on others to provide or help us—are love and belonging and self-esteem or a healthy sense of who we are.

Running through all of these needs is autonomy, or the ability to choose how we will meet these needs. And this freedom is unique to humans. If we have been conditioned not to choose, and thus have a crippling script, we can start evaluating everything we do. Start with the way we get up in the morning. If I usually get up feeling lousy, try changing that—be like Victor Frankl and say to yourself, "One thing that no one can take from me, is my ability to choose what kind of mood I want to have." If he could wake up positive while in prison in the winter in Poland, you and I can do it now in this country.

I found this list of attitudes toward change on a bulletin board:

I don't like where I'm at in life.

I want a new outcome to my actions, but I don't want to exert the effort.

I will try—I might change.

I will do my best.

I'll do whatever it takes.

Of course I hope you're into the last one. I firmly believe that we need to experiment with making and using life-giving choices. That is, choices that are good for us and for others. For example, stealing from others to meet our hunger or shelter needs, is not a life-giving choice for us or for others (with some exceptions such as in *Les Miserables*). I have met some thieves, but never a happy one. I've counseled people who totally rely on others to meet their dependency needs, and again, I've never met one who is happy.

MAKING EVERYDAY CHOICES THAT HELP US LIVE HAPPILY

Life has many experiences that easily help us to be happy—falling in love, getting a new and good job, getting a raise, joining in at a joyous party, and many other events. And everyday life also has many experiences that are stressful and sometimes, tragic. They are not events or experiences that make us or anyone else happy. Even with these problems, we can decide how we want to handle them.

One way of looking at these problems is to see them as type 1, 2 and 3. A type 1 problem is an everyday kind of problem like burning the toast, leaving the house unlocked and having to go back and lock it; tearing a new pair of pants, and so on. The type 1 is basically an inconvenience and is not permanently damaging.

A type 2 problem is more serious, such as breaking a leg, getting sick with a severe cold or flu or some other illness, getting fired from a job or getting evicted from our apartment, and many more events that are serious but recoverable. Even a divorce or bankruptcy, though very stressful, is an experience we can recover from.

Type 3 problems are ones in which there is no recovery—a terminal illness, suicide, homicide, sentence to life imprisonment, and other catastrophes.

Our choices come from how we deal with these problems. Positive and mature people treat type 1 problems for what they are—inconveniences. I can say, "Okay, damnit I have to go back home and make sure the house is locked. I'm going to be more careful next time, but I'm not going to let it ruin my day." "What am I going to do with these torn pants?" I had this happen once while I was teaching—I taught from the chair rather than roaming around. I wasn't happy but I didn't let it ruin my day or week.

There are many people, and I'm sure you know some of them, who seem to have a script that makes them think that every little type 1 problem is a type 2 or even 3. "Oh, my god, what I am going to do, I put on the wrong color blouse and it will just embarrass me to death." And they act like they are near death—from the way they are carrying on. As they see the world, they just cannot be happy because something is going wrong all of the time.

It took me years to learn not to sweat the small stuff—and to notice that a great deal of what we have to deal with is small stuff. One early lesson for me came one morning when I had an appointment in a town thirty-five miles away and too many important things to do before I left. I ended up with twenty minutes to drive the thirty-five miles and find a place to park. I was on the freeway and choking the steering wheel until my knuckles were white. I then realized I wouldn't get there any faster by getting painfully tense. I relaxed and enjoyed the scenery and was fifteen minutes late to the meeting. And guess what? The world didn't come to an end. Up to that time in my life, I was often scurrying around and driving myself and everyone around me quite batty. I decided I'd rather be happy than batty. A question we might ask ourselves is this: "Am I driving, or being driven?" When I'm driving, I'm choosing and in control; when I've driven, I'm being pushed by some habitual way of thinking and behaving that I don't even think about but which is running my life. Meditation, and simply ruminating about life and the world I live in, can be helpful.

If we have gotten into the habit of being relaxed and happy and some serious and tragic event happens, it would be abnormal to express our feelings in a joyful or jovial manner. However, our habit of approaching life in a positive way could help us as we work through the stressful event. And probably, we would be in a position to help others who are also involved. For example, if we have an accident and need to go to the hospital, we will survive best, if we can relax, be patient with ourselves, our family members, and the hospital staff. Learning to make positive responses take practice, especially if we come from a family, as I have, which seems to enjoy being angry and insensitive— and depressed. More on that last sentence later.

So, practice making decisions many times a day and often ask yourself, "What is the best way to handle this?" This takes a great deal of self-control and patience and these two virtues—stopping and asking—are two good habits we need to learn and/or strengthen.

Now, let's look at one of our most basic choices—choosing or declining to accept ourselves—warts, gifts and all—in chapter three.

Chapter 3

KNOWING AND ACCEPTING OURSELVES

Know thyself and to thy self be true.

Shakespeare

When you grow up thinking you are nobody, to be anybody, you need to be somebody else.

Marilyn Monroe—
when asked why she
became an actress.

ON SELF ACCEPTANCE

The more I think about knowing myself, the more complicated it seems. I, and everyone else, started life in union with another person— mother. We are one with our mother while in the womb and only gradually become a separate self after birth. That sense of being in union with another person stays, throughout our lives, no matter how independent we become—or think we've become. As mentioned before, we begin being ourselves in our mother's womb. Hopefully it was a good place and not a toxic place. In any event, here we are in the world—for better or for worse. And we have some say about whether or not it will be a good place for us.

Take a moment to reflect on your own history—your script. Were you encouraged to be your independent self, or were you encouraged to be dependent on your mother or your father, or both? Did they encourage you to increasingly make your own decisions or were you supposed to check with them about nearly everything even through high school? I once counseled a young man who had extreme anxiety when he was alone. When he was in high school, he could not even look into the refrigerator without his mother supervising what he was doing. Along with his anxiety, he was also depressed about life, and had low self-esteem. Self-esteem grows as we increasingly accept ourselves in more and more activities and with many different people.

We develop our scripts and our prejudices and this idea is well presented in the musical, *South Pacific,* with Rodgers and Hammerstein's insightful song about children being scripted:

> *You've got to be taught to be afraid*
> *Of people whose eyes are oddly made.*
> *Of people whose skin is a different shade.*
> *You've got to be carefully taught.*
> *You've got to be taught before it's too late,*
> *Before you are six or seven or eight,*
> *To hate all the people your relatives hate.*
> *You've got to be carefully taught.*

If you have been carefully taught some of this, take a look and see if this is what you want in your life and in your current or future family. Because we are naturally loving and accepting beings, I believe we must let go of prejudices and teachings that prevent us from connecting with others. If I want to live with myself and enjoy it, then it is a must.

There is an opposite script and that is that we are left with too little guidance about what to do and what to think. An example of this would be a young woman whom I counseled years ago. She never knew her father and her mother was a drug addict, so she had to be her mother's keeper. She did amazingly well until she was a teen and fell for a young man who was involved in a gang consisting of school drop-outs and made a living selling drugs. She was anxious, depressed and lost. Fortunately, she was quite intelligent and was open to reading books that had very positive values and guidelines. I recommended

Scott Peck's *The Road Less Traveled*, which she read and carried around with her. She started working on her GED and enrolled in community college. She created a better script for herself. I don't know how her story unfolded but I do know that she entered her following phase with a sparkle in her eyes.

One thing seems certain, none of us will ever be perfect, for we are finite, limited and breakable beings. And even though I believe we are all gifted and wonder-filled, we grow imperfectly. A hundred years ago, western society, with its many restrictions—especially for women—tended to create a great deal of negative emotional reactions to nearly everything. In our times, with so much instability and mobility, we tend to be afflicted with what is called borderline personality disorder—characterized by our finding it difficult to develop a clear identity and feeling "at home" any place. This would be in contrast to earlier times when a child tended to grow up to be much like his or her parents of the same sex and create a life much like theirs. Now nearly all of us have the freedom, the challenge, and the burden of discovering who we are—to find our true integrated center.

One of my mentors, Dr. Erving Polster, wrote a book, *Every Person's Life is Worth A Novel*. I would amend it to state, every person's life is worth several novels. I have been sharing with you part of my own life's "novel" or journey in the hope that you have begun to reflect on your own.

ACCETANCE AND MY OWN JOURNEY

I now think of my mother as having been quite heroic for not only surviving many hardships but continuing to care for her eight children as well. In my early years I resented her for giving most of her attention to my youngest sister who was a "blue baby" and thus brain-damaged. I concluded, by the time I was four years old, that I would have to take care of myself, if I was to survive. This led to the challenge of being unhealthily independent, but still yearning to belong in a special way to someone. I could say that I was scripted to be a loner.

In the western world, we are encouraged to develop our individuation—or independent self. I often think that we have gone too far, even to the point of being isolated and out of touch with others—and thus depressed. As Dr. Maslow stated, our love and belonging need is one of our basic needs—like food, water, and safety. Around the time I first read *The Cipher In The Snow* mentioned in chapter 1, I realized that I had despised my young self and had worked to forget him. I had ingested my dad's words that I was "a worthless piece of shit." I knew, theoretically, that we need to accept our life experiences, but that article and my tears directed me to accept that part of myself. I knew that lonely little boy still resides in me. He is a part of me.

ACCEPTING OUR DIFFERENT "PARTS"

Every person's journey to maturity and wholeness involves accepting our exploratory self as we grow through the years. And our exploratory self has many parts. Hopefully one part is a daring self who explores different ways of being. We may decide to do various things and then realize that many of those things we chose were mistakes—but were also learning experiences. Hopefully, we make many decisions, at least as many as our parents and other caregivers allow.

During my second year in South Dakota, I learned a great deal by carefully observing everything Dad did—from carpentry, to waiting on customers, and talking to people. That, and my teacher, Ms. Reed, thinking I was smart, helped me to begin adding some positive "parts" to my sense of self. I was a good worker and a good student. It was years later that I learned that one never becomes somebody because of what they do but because of who they are—when a person realizes he or she is someone just because they *are*!

TRYING TO BE GOOD ENOUGH

When I was fourteen, my dad died. My world crumbled. The only person who really thought I was important and thought I could become a priest was gone. At the same time, I was happy not having him around to tell me what to do all of the time. I threw the ugly hat he made me wear into the corner and let it collect dust. I hated wearing hats after that for my entire life.

I wanted to stay working at the lumber yard, and my brother Jim, just out of the Navy, joined me there. Again, I was important because I knew more about the business than he did. My mother and sisters came back to our small town. I helped pay the grocery bill. I still wanted to be a priest but decided that I would wait until I had helped Mom like my older brothers had done. I decided that I needed to help my youngest sister graduate from high school. I was not an adolescent who played around, I was a responsible man who worked and paid bills. I would be good, and that meant not do anything sexual at all or even think about it, and work hard and study hard and someday I would be somebody. I would be a priest who would not be hurtful to little kids. Father Groel was kind and gentle like that and I served Mass for him every day for five years. I decided to take high school in three years, so I could get to the seminary more quickly. No one told me to do this nor to study and work hard. I was free to do what I wanted and I did.

We moved to Wichita, Kansas when I was sixteen and in the middle of my sophomore year. I found work at a lumber yard and completed high school in three years by taking seven courses in my senior year—while working thirty hours a week at the lumber company.

I graduated as the boy with the highest GPA in the class with seventy guys. One of the most memorable things about graduation in 1951 was that the owners of the lumber company came to my class's honors night and saw me receive an "outstanding student" award for finishing high school in three years with an A-B average. Maybe, I thought, I really could be somebody.

Needing To Belong

Right after high school and at age eighteen, the owners of the lumber yard made me the assistant manager. I worked extra hours that summer, and managed to buy a small house for Mom, two sisters and myself. I then built a rental house in the back when I was twenty-one and made it to the seminary when I was twenty-three. I thought I was a pretty good hard-working guy. I never thought I was driven—even though I had rather constant headaches—I just did what I wanted and needed to do. I did overhear occasionally that I was a "cold fish" or "unfeeling" or "had ice-water in my veins." Was that bad? I kept on being driven. I had never been invited to birthday parties or any other kind of social gatherings like other kids and fellows. I was often very lonely but pretended I didn't need anyone—and everyone got the message that I was not available.

So I arrived at early adulthood, or late adolescence, thinking I was quite mature and a man. If anyone asked me if I knew myself, I don't know what I would have said, but I imagine I would have said, "Yep, I do."

I felt like a mature young man, but I also thought I was different from other young fellows. I envied the guys who could play a musical instrument—especially a piano or guitar. I never had time to play sports or have a coach and so with pickup games of baseball, tag football or basketball, I was usually chosen last. The ones I really envied were the

guys who had a way with girls and dated the prettiest cheerleaders.
I pretended that I wasn't interested because I was planning to be a
priest. Of course, I was just kidding myself.

As we work to develop our
sense of self, it is important to
evaluate the different people, ideas,
and values that have influenced us.
An example of this need was vividly
pointed out to me last year. Two
very different college women came
in for counseling. They sought
help because of their depression.
The first, age nineteen, stated
that she was depressed because
she was too short at five foot, one
inch. She came from a wealthy
family and her parents had paid
for several cosmetic surgeries but
refused to pay for a trip to Europe
for leg-lengthening surgery. It
cost $80,000 plus expenses. At the
first visit she said she "hated" her

parents. She resisted the idea of going deeper in her thinking. She
did seem to make some progress but stopped therapy after only eight
sessions. The other young woman had the opposite problem, she was
too tall at five feet, eleven inches. She hated standing out in every
crowd. It helped her when I told her that many star models were about
as tall as she was. Of course, like the other woman, she needed to look
deeper into her self and, in some way, realize that every person's real
self-worth is based on their ability to love, create and just "be." Both of
these young women had a belief that they must be physically "perfect"
if they wished to be accepted in life.

I, too, spent much of my early life feeling varying degrees of depression. In my forties I decided to seek help from a therapist. I told him my story and when I mentioned my early work ethic and helping my mom, the therapist said, "I imagine that your brothers and sisters really appreciated all that you did." I immediately started to cry and said, "If they did appreciate it, they never told me." So my rather radical independence had a steep price—and it took me years to realize it. I had acted like I really didn't need help from anyone for anything. In other words, I had pushed my siblings away by not asking for help. I am still working on letting go of that stubborn need to be radically independent. The life-giving need to love and be loved is far more important.

No matter how old you are, give your own youth a hard look and know and accept those parts of yourself that you have neglected. In the next chapter we'll take a deeper look into this important concept—after all, keep in mind that every person's life is worth a novel—including yours.

Chapter 4

OWNING AND TELLING OUR STORIES

The reason there is evil in the world is because people don't get to tell their stories.

Carl Jung

*Though summer turns to winter and the present disappears
the laughter we were glad to share will echo through the years.*

Song: Moments to
Remember by Allen
and Stillman

TELLING OUR STORIES

I definitely agree with the great psychoanalyst, Carl Jung, that when a person tells his whole story and is listened to, he becomes more accepting of himself, which leads more easily to the accepting of others. The story-telling allows a person to let go of anger, bitterness, and evil or hurtful intentions. Our story, or script, is often so sad and even bitter, we want to forget it—not tell it. I know that was the way I felt for years, but when I began accepting myself more completely and began telling my story, I began to feel better. And as a counselor, when people begin telling me about their experiences in emotional detail, they begin to understand and accept themselves more and even begin enjoying life. At the same time, they began to change their script. It is remarkable that the more that is shared the more livable life becomes.

The song, *Moments to Remember*, tells us that the laughter we experienced is gladly shared. The writers wanted a happy song, so they did not say that the shame, the mistakes, and sad times are more easily remembered but often nearly impossible to share. It is the *tears we want to hide are, too often, what echoes through the years.* Perhaps, recalling the good times is a way of helping us keep going and eventually makes it possible to work through the doubts as we struggle to find our true selves. Depressed people often are able to see only the darkness they have experienced and have allowed these experiences to define who they are.

Every life-giving person I've known well has gone through 'the fiery furnace' of sadness, hurt, grief, or failure. When they dig deep within themselves, often with the help of a counselor, they will begin to harness the tremendous courage and patience that is available to us as humans. They will emerge as persons who more easily understand love, are brave, and hope for themselves and others. As we tell our whole story, we begin changing our script, and begin panning for gold—that is, to find the good times we have had, the successes we have experienced, and to recall the people we have loved along the way. You would not be alive and be reading this if you had not experienced some positive times in your life.

Overcoming A Bad Beginning And Learning To Grow

I avoided much of my early sadness and hurt by escaping into work. Another escape was to fantasize a future that would be rosier and I spent hours and years in that fantasy. A positive and prominent role in my young life was my dog Pal; he was the supportive gold during my first eight years of life, just as work and dreaming were in later years.

I continued to leave my emotional life unexamined by carrying my work-aholism into college and the seminary. My freshman year, not knowing any better, I let the college registrar enroll me in seven courses, for a total of 24 semester units. Being the only one in my family to go to college, I didn't know a class unit from an apple. A few classmates told me that it was ridiculous, but I managed—it was much easier than the 80 hour work-week I was used to. It allowed me to keep so busy, I didn't have time to ponder my history of sadness and depression. To my surprise and my classmates, I made the honor roll—3.8 GPA. Even then, 1 wasn't sure I was smart enough to be a priest. That darned script hadn't changed yet.

My first year of college was in a Catholic liberal arts college and my second year was my first year in a seminary proper. I studied with a great bunch of guys, but really didn't get to know them as well as I could have—if I had gained the skill of forming good friendships earlier. I did keep busy. A typical year involved taking 18-21 semester units of courses and I added working at the book bindery (later as a manager), formed a Toastmaster club, became associate editor of the schools magazine, and became the school cabinet maker. I did make time to play handball and other sports about three times a week. It took a year to convince myself that these athletic activities were not a waste of time.

It wasn't until years later, when I got an education in psychology, worked with people in counseling, that I began to experience the deep feelings that I had buried my entire life. One of my earliest educational experiences helped me understand the necessity of working through early trauma. During an experiential seminar, I mentioned that I was the only one of eight children who lived with my dad the last years of his life. The therapist asked me to tell the group about what that was like. When I got to fourteen, the time of Dad's death, I broke down in tears—probably for the first time since he had died 26 years earlier.

I said to the group, "I had come home from school at lunch time and found the lumberyard locked up. I went to the bungalow and found Dad in bed. He was so sick he couldn't move. I called my brothers in a neighboring town and they came over and we took him to the hospital 28 miles away. I insisted on staying in the hospital room with Dad. I was so determined that they put a cot in the room for me. One of the nurses showed me how to take Dad's pulse while holding his wrist. Dad was in a coma, and I stayed by his bedside and held his wrist for six days, only breaking for a little sleep at night and going to the bathroom. I was holding his hand and feeling his pulse on the sixth day when his pulse seemed to disappear."

I had made it that far in my recitation before I started crying. I did my best to stymie the tears and brokenly continued, "I pushed the "call" button and a nurse came in and confirmed that Dad's heart had stopped. She said, "I'm sorry, Donald, your dad has died."

I screamed, "Dad, don't leave me. Dad don't go." The nurse put her hand on my shoulder and I pushed it off and said, "Go away, you're not helping." I put my head on the bed and cried.

I looked around at the therapist and my fellow seminar students. I felt I had so embarrassed myself, I wanted to run from the room. I stayed and sat there in the group feeling ashamed of my tears and my "weakness." Fortunately for me, the therapist was exceedingly supportive—mostly by just being there for me and not talking, for it seemed a long time. I am crying as I write this and I am glad that I am feeling—yes, just that—I'm feeling. I didn't cry at Dad's funeral and shed more tears for him when I was forty than ever in my life. It was then that I learned that tears are an appropriate and healthy expression of our pain and a discharge of grief. And there is no time-line for feeling grief. I didn't cry at Dad's funeral because I was too angry at my siblings who sat there bawling, even though they hadn't even sent him a Christmas or birthday card for years. My tears at my dad's funeral were twenty-six years late.

THE IMPORTANCE OF REMEMBERING

Whenever we act like we don't feel sadness, grief, anger or any other emotion and let it fester underground, we hurt ourselves. Unexpressed and hidden feelings are still there and if we don't deal with them, they will bite us in the heart, and prevent us from enjoying our life and easily connecting with others. Unfortunately, I now know that there are millions of others who did, and do, the same thing I did. Our scripts demand that we—especially males—stifle it.

I would like to share the stories of three people whose trauma was far worse than mine but who did find relief by telling their stories. I was deeply touched by them. I will disguise their identities so that they alone, if they are alive and reading this, might know who I am discussing. I've told each of them that they should give themselves a pat on the back for, if nothing else, surviving. They have each earned a Purple Heart.

One of my first counselees was a very depressed woman in her forties. She had seen several therapists before, but for some reason never revealed the trauma of her childhood. She was the twelfth child of a poor family who lived in the slum section of a large east coast city. For weeks, she refused to talk about her family and her childhood. I kept insisting, and told her it was important, if she were to successfully emerge from her depression. She had been what she called betrayed so many times that she trusted no one. "And, besides," she said, "that's all past and I have worked hard to forget all about it." I kept insisting that we do not really forget anything we have experienced. Finally she began to disclose, through many tears, her painful early years. She had been repeatedly raped by two of her older brothers as a young girl. After the first time, she told her mother, hoping that she would do something to stop the boys. Instead of making any kind of disciplinary intervention, her mother beat her with a knotted rope until she bled—and threatened her with more if she ever lied like that again. The rape continued.

I was told this story over forty years ago and I am still shedding tears as I am writing about it now. It does have a positive ending however. She did find some gold in her horrible early years—she was intelligent and strong. She decided that she wanted to live and to succeed in life. She went to college and then to graduate school, obtained a Ph.D, and became a psychotherapist. I hired her as an Intern. She was a gifted therapist until she retired. Even though the shadow of her childhood never disappeared—she had turned her haunts into memories. All the anti-depressants she had taken before she saw me, did not help her. She needed to expose her personal history and accept it as just that: history. The pain and process was necessary for her and she learned to enjoy being herself and being alive.

The old saying, "Forgive and forget," is incorrect. It should be changed to: "forgive and *accept*," because we do not forget anything. To accept does not mean that whatever happened was good or forgotten, but that we accept that it is part of our history. We can make it a memory and not a haunt that tortures us. We can put it on one of our mind's "back burners" and not bring it into our conscious mind's foreground, but it is still there and will bite us and ruin our lives, unless we can turn those haunts into memories. That is why we must accept our history, if we hope to enjoy ourselves.

I had another client with a devastating past he had kept in a closet for decades. It refused to stay hidden after a disabling industrial accident forced him to bring it to light. He could no longer escape into his time-consuming work-aholism because of his injuries. He scheduled therapy, thinking he could simply get a pill to reduce his severe depression. An anti-depressant was prescribed along with counseling. It took him nearly six weeks to disclose some of the childhood trauma that he could no longer ignore. His parents were alcoholics and drug addicts and when he was between the ages of five and seven they began torturing him. Several times a week they would hang him up in a door frame and take turns beating him until he passed out or they got too tired or too spaced out to continue. This went on until a neighbor reported the screaming in the house to the police. Of course he cried and continued to cry during and after the months of therapy. Often, I cried with him—it was impossible not to feel with his grief. By telling his story and accepting his history, he is finding the gold in his heart. He continues with less frequent therapy and now helps others in a homeless shelter and, although continuing to be haunted, is beginning to enjoy life.

Sometimes, it is the feelings of guilt and shame that we need to expose and wrestle with in the light of day—or light of therapy. An example of this would be a woman whom I worked with many years ago. She was, and is, a very intelligent person who was outwardly happily married and at that time with four young children. She was very depressed and came to counseling thinking it was just the stress of being a full time homemaker and mother. For a few weeks, we took a look at her feelings, thoughts and activities. It all seemed too inconsequential to be the cause of her severe depression and so, after four weeks, I said, "For some reason, I think there is something in your life that is very important but which you haven't shared with me."

At the time she said, "No, I don't think so. I've covered pretty much everything." A few weeks later she said, "Remember the time you said there was something important that I haven't told you?" I nodded and she stalled for several more minutes and then blurted out, "When I was twenty and twenty-one, I worked as a prostitute." She stared at me with eyes wide open as if expecting me to react in some negative way.

I blurted out, "I'll be damned. So was I."

"What do you mean, so were you?" She was incredulous.

"I was a Catholic priest." I had never told her that before.

"What's that got to do with me—with what I just told you?"

"You were doing something that was unnatural for you, and I was doing something that was unnatural for me." I had never explicitly thought this, but I think it came to me at that moment because I had often thought that a life of celibacy was unnatural—at least for me.

She opened her eyes even wider and then started laughing. We both laughed until tears started flowing down our cheeks. She then said, "Well, at least yours was more socially acceptable!" Later she told me that was the most helpful and liberating thing anyone had ever said to her. "You saved my life," she said. We both found some gold in ourselves that day. She later ran for public office and won several elections over the years. She found her true self and became a person who began to enjoy life. Again, no pill could have done that for her.

So, we often need to forgive and *accept* ourselves too. One of my prejudices is toward 'holier-than-thou' kind of people who act like they have never done a bad thing, or experienced a single failure, in their lives. They tend to look down their noses at we mortals who do hurtful and life-diminishing things. And I am always suspicious of the "perfect" ones who blame everyone around them for any mistakes they make or negative feelings they have.

No one is perfect and we all do feel some, or a lot of, shame and guilt because of things we have done it the past. If I hurt a child, I should feel guilty and I should "be ashamed of myself." Because of shame and guilt I may be motivated to become a more kind and loving person. They are not always useless feelings. At the same time, I think parents, teachers, and ministers too often lay shame and guilt on children and young people.

Hopefully, most of us have not had such traumatic, and dramatic, experiences as the three persons mentioned above, but everyone has had experiences we are not proud of or so hurtful we can't stand the thought of talking about them to anyone. I applaud Dr. Brene Brown's (book: *The Gift of Our Imperfections)* idea that we need to be grateful for our imperfections, for they allow us, if we have the courage, to be engaged with and compassionate toward others.

Accept, and be proud of your accomplishments. It is necessary to recognize and be proud of what we've done that is positive—starting with survival. As we continually become at ease with ourselves and basically satisfied with life and ourselves, we can relax and just enjoy being ourselves. Until that time—usually in the second half of our lives, it is necessary in order to discover who we are. So own your history—both good and bad—and become flourishingly human.

As Carl Jung said, "The reason there is evil in the world is because people don't get to tell their stories." So add your name to the list of those who do tell their stories—it will change your script.

Chapter 5

NOT GIVING OUR MINDS AWAY

No man can reveal to you aught but that which already lies half asleep in the dawning of your knowledge. If he is indeed wise he does not bid you enter the house of his wisdom, but rather leads you to the threshold of your own mind.

Kahlil Gibran,
The Prophet

DISCOVERING YOUR OWN MIND

You cannot give something away if you do not have it. So I hope you have your own mind and know it is really yours and not someone else's. It took me at least as long to find my own mind as it did to find my true self—in fact, I'm still working on both. I now believe that each undertaking is a life-long search. I know I enjoy living with myself when I am thinking for myself.

It has taken me years to believe that my own thoughts and my own solutions to problems were as good as, if not better, than someone else's. Working at the lumber yard and doing remodeling on the side helped me learn to figure out how to do things without relying on someone else. I had enough confidence in my ability to work and make enough money to make house payments when I was eighteen, allowing me, as I mentioned, to buy a house for Mom, my youngest sister, and myself. At that time, the sister two years older than me got engaged to an intelligent fellow who was a confirmed atheist. I was still planning to become a priest, so I polished my debating ability with my future brother-in-law. I even used some of his arguments with seminary professors, years later. I was developing a mind of my own, but I still deferred to those whom I thought were smarter than me like book authors and professors. My script included the fear that I was stupid as well as ignorant. I might win an argument with my brother-in-law but I dared not challenge the more learned ones.

When I started college, because I was unsure of myself, I just followed what was presented by professors and in books. I did feel resentful about being treated like a child. We even had an unfunny joke: The way to make a priest out of a young man was to dress him like a girl (the cassock) and treat him like a boy for eight years. There were some 25 bells a day, telling us where to go and what to do. One day, I was managing the work of ten to twelve men and the next day I was a little boy being told what to do nearly every moment of the day. I almost left the seminary. Then I decided that I didn't care if they asked me to crawl through horse shit every morning, I was going to be a priest. And when I was ordained, I could think for myself and be myself.

Wrong! I soon learned that being an obedient priest was not only going where the bishop asked me to go, but to think the same way he did. For him and for the centuries-old Church, there were absolute truths and ways of doing everything. It was like the military. I thought that maybe if I work hard and conformed in most ways, I could gain more freedom. I read Erich Hoffer's book, *The True Believer,* and realized that his description fitted me too well. A true believer, according to Hoffer, is someone who follows dictates without question. To better learn my job as diocesan religious education director and to widen my understanding of myself, I enrolled in a summer graduate program in religious education at Loyola University in Chicago.

The very first professor said that the human being is like a helicopter—the big prop in the front lifts the plane off the ground and keeps it moving, the small prop in the back gives it direction.

A person's emotions are the big prop and his intellect is the small prop that gives him direction. I loved the idea but thought, *I'm not a helicopter; I'm an army tank.* I lost out on both accounts, my mind had been hijacked by Church officials and traditional teachings and I had never let my emotions get me off the ground.

GIVE YOURSELF PERMISSION TO DECIDE WHAT YOU THINK AND WANT TO DO

I decided to give my emotions a little freedom that summer. I had learned a Greek folk dance from a group of volunteers before leaving Wichita and I had taken a record with me. A room in our dorm was set aside for a graduate student pub. We rounded up a record player and I started teaching priests and nuns the folk dance. I was nicknamed Zorba and had the best time of my life. I was becoming a helicopter— and beginning to be my true self.

My teaching and my sermons became more interesting and lively. I asked a beautiful nun to help me teach teachers. Of course, I picked her because she was an excellent teacher and was also in a Master's program in theology. Her beauty had nothing to do with it (And if you believe that, I'll sell you a bridge in New York). I was living with myself and enjoying it—for the first time in my life.

Then one day, after several months of teaching together, this beautiful and very intelligent nun stopped me as we walked across a parking lot, and said, "Don, I have something important to tell you."

I turned to her, "What's that?"

Very quietly and sincerely, she said, "Don, I love you."

I froze for a moment. Part of me was scared to death—she couldn't love me, she didn't really know me because if she did know me, she'd take that back. Maybe she's not as intelligent as I thought. The other part of me wanted to dance down the street like Gene Kelly. After a full two minutes, I solemnly said, "Uh, thank you." I wasn't a complete iceberg, and six weeks later I told her that I had been in love with her for months. And three years later, I asked her to marry me—and that was 45 years ago and she is still putting up with me.

WE NEED SUPPORT PEOPLE AS WE DEVELOP OUR OWN MIND

Having someone so absolutely wonderful, beautiful and intelligent love me, gave me the courage to express my real thoughts—my own mind. With that I listened more. Some months later, I was leading a seminar with a group of teachers, all nuns, and we would begin our sessions with Mass. We went to the convent chapel for that. After two or three weeks, one of the participants said, "Why don't we just stay at the table and you can celebrate Mass—and you don't need to wear all the vestments." I asked all of them if that was OK with them. They all said yes, so, with just a stole over my shoulders as a vestment, I celebrated Mass at the dining room table. It was delightful and solemn.

One teacher lied; she was not comfortable with it and informed the bishop about my misbehavior. The bishop called me into his office. He was the nervous type and I could tell he was going to scold me about something. Solemnly, he said, "Father Hanley, I understand that you celebrated Mass without all of the proper vestments. Is that correct?"

I was irritated at the nun who lied and at the bishop who was such a stuffed shirt. I replied, "Yes, I did."

"And Father Hanley, do you think that you know more than the Sacred Congregation of Faith in Rome?"

I knew what he wanted me to say and that was that I had erred and I would never do it again, but I said, "For a small group of nuns in Wichita, Kansas, yes bishop, I believe I do."

He turned a beautiful shade of purple, shook all over and I was afraid he would have a heart attack. He nearly screamed my condemnation, "Father Hanley, you are a free thinker! Get out of my office right now."

I left as angry as he. That was in 1967—in the middle of the Vietnam War and the civil-rights movement. My heroes were the war protesters, Fathers Dan and Phillip Berrigan, civil rights leader Martin Luther King, and advocate for the poor, Dorothy Day, and here I was being called on the carpet for not wearing a few freaking vestments for a private Mass. I thought that it was no wonder the Church was losing credibility for so many.

It took me two or three days to realize that the bishop had given me a wonderful gift—an emancipation proclamation—I was a **free thinker**. For the first time in my life, I realized I really did have a mind of my own.

WHAT TAKES ME AND EVERYONE ELSE SO LONG?

I believe our culture is changing and letting go of the idea that there are absolute truths about nearly everything, but it is slow. There are many who still teach and many more want to have absolute answers. "What must I believe and what must I do to get to have success in life? Or get to heaven?" From the moment we are born, we are dependent on others for our very survival. So we assume that our caregivers must know what is important for us to survive. And, too often, our caregivers act like they absolutely do know what is best for us. The key words here are *act* and *absolute*. It is helpful, of course, when the parent and caregivers are confident, themselves, in their own

ability to think and problem solve. When they are confident, they will usually allow the children to have their own thoughts and dialogue about things with them. The confident parent can have a dialogue with the child about the question, "Where do babies come from?"

The most far-reaching revolution of our time is the change from believing that all "facts" are absolute and unchanging, to realizing that everything is in a progressive flux. In the early part of the twentieth century only a few scientists and other thinkers knew this. Darwin's theory of evolution, Einstein's theory of relativity, and the thought and research of countless others, have changed our thinking about nearly everything.

Unfortunately, our education, and even common discourse, continues to present ideas in a way that reflects the old pattern of absolutes. And so we demand that students remain silent as we attempt to pour these "truths" into their little heads—and even into the bigger heads of college and graduate students. An example: On my first week in the seminary, and on my very first day of a class in general science the professor started with astronomy and declared that both the moon and the sun were the only two sources of light in our solar system. I was one of four new students in the sophomore class. I looked around at the other twenty-seven students to see if they would say something about this mistaken notion. When no one spoke up, I held up my hand and said, "Father, the moon reflects the sun's light—it is not a self-illuminating body." The professor, rather imperiously, said, "Are you contradicting me, young man?" I responded, "I don't mean to be insulting, Father, but I do believe you are wrong about this." He harrumphed and went on to something else.

After the class period, several of the "old" students informed me that no one ever challenged a teacher in the seminary. I said I would if I thought they were wrong. One responded, "Well, I hope you don't get kicked out." Fortunately for me, the professor apologized to me at the next class. We later learned that he had a "nervous breakdown" the previous year and was just recovering. I became less challenging, knowing that. The system was still wrong. I continued being cautiously challenging and only one professor years later threatened me with expulsion. I did keep quiet in his class because my goal was to be ordained a priest.

A constant dialogue about "facts," theories, procedures, and everything should be ordinary procedure from kindergarten on up through graduate school. And the constant, and I believe wrong-headed, demand for standardized testing indicates that we still have a long way to go. Respect, openness, sensitivity, curiosity, and inspiration, should be the only constants. Then we all will be keeping our own minds and nurturing our own and others.

Conformity comes from fear and we are taught to be afraid of many things almost from the day we are born—and definitely from the day we begin to talk and to become mobile. "Don't say that!" Do you remember the first time you said the f –bomb? I do because I bit my mom's finger when she tried to wash out my mouth with soap. I had two things to feel guilty about. If you remember, I'm sure you thought the world, or your life, was going to come to an end. You also learned if you want to hear an adult scream, all you need to do is yell the "F" word. That, of course, doesn't really make sense. Hearing a scream when your mother sees you start to run out into the street does make sense.

Fear is natural for our survival, but inordinate fear can freeze us into immobility. There is no place on earth where we can hide from fear but we can spend a lifetime trying to find it anyway.

We can foster the illusion that we are stronger than fear. Amassing a fortune so that we will never face want or hunger or failure is an illusion. We can hide into alcohol, heroin, or some drug, but we know that will only be a temporary fix. We even call it a fix. There is only one force more powerful than fear—and that is love. We'll explore that more thoroughly later.

Religious orders, military institutions, and all organizations should ask for cooperation from everyone and not demand blind obedience. That is, if they want the best and most creative thinking and most life-giving environment in their agency or institution.

We should not follow a teacher or leader who is unjust, unkind, or cruel, even if, in some way appealing to some base prejudice of ours. I still shudder at the newsreels of people saluting Hitler and I still wonder what they were thinking. And I wonder what people were thinking here in our country when they applauded President Bush's invasion of Iraq—76% of Americans favored the invasion when it was happening. I personally believe they were giving their minds away. And if you disagree with me, and we happen to meet, I'll be happy to dialogue with you about it.

I am hopeful when I reflect on some of the changes in consciousness over the past few centuries. Slavery is no longer legal nor practiced in most of the world and where it is practiced it is considered wrong and something to be abolished. A large percentage of people throughout the world accept gay, lesbian and transgender people. Racism is receding and generally condemned by educated people. More and more people are searching for a deeper meaning to life than just acquiring more material stuff. Peace among nations and peoples is no longer seen as just more magical thinking. With all this, more and more people are thinking for themselves rather than looking to others to give them answers.

So let us all keep our own counsel and, at the same time, be open to other's opinions and discoveries. Our own minds must be nurtured in order to be a healthy part of our being. An old Buddhist saying fits here: "If you find your Buddha in the road, kill him." It means, be your own best teacher and don't rely on someone else to do your thinking for you. I would add—do a lot of ruminating—that is, pondering everything. It is a healthy remedy for boredom.

Chapter 6

BEING STRONG ENOUGH TO BE GENTLE

Unless, like the lily, we can rise pure and strong above sordid surroundings, we would probably be moral weaklings in any situation.
Helen Keller

There is a gravitas in the second half of life ... Life is much more spacious now, the boundaries of the container have been enlarged by the constant addition of new experiences and relationships.
Richard Rohr

BEING STRONG ENOUGH TO BE GENTLE

In my younger years, if someone called me a pure and strong lily, I probably would have punched him in the mouth. Now I can understand Helen Keller's words as meaning the same thing as being strong enough to be gentle. Richard Rohr's idea that, as we grow older, we are enlarged by experiences and relationships with others. If we have altered our script to include being open and caring, this will happen rather automatically and we need not wait until the second half of life.

Having read this far, I hope you are choosing to be accepting of yourself and your history. I also hope you are aware of, and taking responsibility for, your own thoughts and actions—not giving your mind away. So your new script now includes discovering the gift of your strengths, as well as your imperfections and vulnerability. In my youth and early, and even middle, adulthood, I rarely, if ever, allowed myself to feel or express weakness—it wasn't manly or even human. Now, in my eighties, I still automatically think of myself as strong. Of course, I have to admit that it is not true, at least physically, when I ask my wife or someone to open the jar of pickles or pick up anything over three pounds.

Being realistic about our strengths and weaknesses at any age makes us strong enough NOT to feel the need to have power over another person or persons. It was liberating for me to find myself able to own my own power and to celebrate others' power *with* them. Again, I ask you to think of some of my heroes, such as Nelson Mandela, Mohandas Ghandi, Helen Keller, and Maya Angelou. They were strong enough to be gentle and lived it. As I am revising this chapter, I witnessed a moving event on television. Chris Paul and the L.A. Clippers had just won the first round of the NBA tournament over the San Antonio Spurs by two points. Tim Duncan, star forward of the Spurs, gave Chris Paul a congratulatory hug and then gently cradled Paul's head to his chest. Both men were gracious in victory and defeat—both were strong and gentle. That, to me, was a true sign of maturity.

Several years ago I worked with a man in his mid-forties who would fit the description of a "man's man"—muscular, square jaw, determined looking and tough. His opening remark was, "I want you to help me NOT kill a man." He had caught his wife in bed with a man. Previously, he had found his first wife in bed with another man and nearly killed the guy. Fortunately, or unfortunately, the other man had not pressed charges for assault. He said he had managed to hold back his temper this time for fear of going to prison. My client realized that there must be something wrong with the way he treated his wife, or wives, that they sought the attention of other men. At the end of our third session, I said, "One of the greatest challenges we have as men is to become strong enough to be gentle."

The next week he came back and the first thing he said was, "You know, Doc, you said that we need to become strong enough to be gentle. I don't have the foggiest idea what it means to be gentle. Will you teach me?"

I was really impressed with his honesty and sincerity. I asked. "Joe, first, tell me what being gentle means to you right now?"

"Well, my first reaction is that being gentle is being a namby-pamby, a sissy or a wimp. But I know that's not what you mean. I haven't told you before, but I grew up in a mafia family in New Jersey with four brothers. I was the youngest and our mom died when I was young." I thought I saw tears forming in his eyes when he mentioned his mom. He went on, "So, you see, I don't know gentle from shit."

The closest I'd ever come to the mafia is the Godfather films, and thought he might have some kind of Catholic upbringing. I asked him about that. He said his mom went to church with him and his brothers every Sunday until her death. He had gone to a Catholic school until he was in the sixth grade, but stopped going to church because his dad never went and didn't care whether the boys went or not.

"Do you think Jesus was a wimp?"

"Naw, but he was God, he could be whatever he wanted to be. Doc, I ain't no Jesus."

"I know, but let's look at Jesus, the man. I think he was a strong man, as well as a gentle man."

"And look what happened to him." He chuckled and went on, "When I was a kid, I wondered why he didn't just kill those Roman bastards. After all, he was God."

"I remember thinking the same thing. Later, I learned that his central message for us was that we are to love one another—and we have the power to do so, if we desire. After spending his life teaching love, what weight do you think his words would have, if he had killed his accusers rather than be executed? Remember, Christian tradition holds that he was fully human too. So, I'll ask again. Was he a wimp?"

"Put that way, I'd guess not. What about his dying for our sins?"

I didn't want to go into more theology or bible studies, so I just said, "Isn't dying to preserve the message the same thing?"

"Okay, yeah, I guess. So tell me, Doc, what about you? Have you ever wanted to kill someone, or at least bust them in the jaw?"

"Yeah, I did. When I was eleven years old, I wanted to kill my dad because he was beating my mom."

"So, what did you do?"

"First, I grabbed his arm, but he backhanded me and knocked me to the floor. Then I ran to get the town marshal, about a block away. By the time we got back, Dad had stopped the beating. They, Dad and the marshal, just talked. Of course, I'm glad I didn't have any kind of weapon to kill my dad."

I went on to tell him that we all needed to be so in touch with thoughts and emotions and be in control of ourselves, even when we feel like killing or hurting others. I used the analogy of the human person being like a helicopter. "The helicopter has the large prop that keeps it up in the air and moves it forward, back, and all. The small prop in back guides the plane. The large prop is our emotions and the small prop is our brain or intellect and that gives us direction. When you felt like killing that fellow, your emotions were driving you, but fortunately for you, your intellect took control—unlike the first time that happened."

"I like that helicopter example. Yer pretty smart, Doc."

"Thank you. So what do you think now about your wife and you?"

"I think I've been a lousy husband or she wouldn't be looking elsewhere. Would you be willing to see both of us, for uh, some marriage counseling?"

We did work together for a few weeks, ending with my tough guy giving his wife a hug and opening his arms for me to join him in an embrace. I did. His wife said,

"You know, Doctor, I'm beginning to think Joe is becoming strong enough to be gentle."

Words Can Also Be Brutal

"Sticks and stones can break my bones, but words can never hurt me." This old saying is as wrong-headed as "Forgive and forget." My broken bones can heal and hurtful words can heal also—but it takes longer and, often, the process is more difficult. A recent, 2015, study reveals that verbal bullying is more harmful to children's self-esteem and mental-emotional health than physical abuse.

Many years ago, I was visiting my sister and her family—husband and four children.

My sister and her husband had stayed up late drinking. I went to bed soon after the children did. I got up with the children and was playing with them when their mother came down the stairs and saw the tossed toys, drawings, crayons and markers all around the family room. It was a delightful mess that I thought could easily be cleaned up. My sister threw a fit and zeroed in on the oldest, twelve year old Theresa, and told her how irresponsible, careless, and thoughtless she was. She ended her tirade with, "You are a selfish, stupid little shit."

I started picking things up and, too angrily, said, "Come on, Sis, we can clean this up in five minutes. Theresa is not selfish and stupid. Get a grip."

"Don't tell me how to talk to my children. You don't have any kids and when you do, you can tell me something. So, get the hell out of my house right now." Unfortunately, she was correct on one thing—

years later, while drinking, I lost control of my anger and hurt my own daughters. I'll share more on that in a later chapter.

Thinking that my continued presence would just add more turmoil, I picked up my bag and headed to the car. All four of the kids followed me out and gave me hugs. As Theresa was giving me a hug, she said, "Uncle Don, did you really mean what you said to mom? That I wasn't stupid and selfish?"

"I certainly did, Theresa. You are a wonderful person and don't let your mom or dad or anyone else tell you otherwise." All five of us were crying as I backed out of the driveway.

Money: Too Often A Weapon Of Power

Years ago, Howard, the husband of a woman I had seen three times in therapy, drove up in what looked like a new Mercedes. When the spouse of a client whom I had already seen joins us in therapy, I take a few minutes to see the new client alone—to establish some kind of rapport, if possible, and ask him or her how they see the marriage.

I was seeing clients at my home office at that time. I saw Howard exit his car, look critically at our house and the neighborhood, then walk toward the office. I could tell that he was disdainful of my home and professional office.

My house is modest, by California standards, but much larger and nicer than any place my parents ever lived—even with eight children. I didn't tell Howard all this. When he got settled down and visually inspected my office, I said "So, Howard, tell me, about your marriage and why you think Cecelia asked you to join us.

"I suppose she told you what a dictatorial bastard I am?"

"No, she said you were not always easy to get along with but you were very intelligent and a good provider." I didn't add that she also called him a control freak and cold as ice. She excused him by saying he had a horrible childhood and wasn't a drunk like his father. Also he never beat the kids like his father did.

"Well, that's good to hear. As you know, she is a beautiful woman and I'm very proud of her when we attend conferences and other business gatherings—and I have quite a few. About a year ago she started being a bit depressed, withdrawn, and often refusing to attend many of my functions. Our youngest started high school and I think she just missed the kids being little and underfoot. She went to a psychiatrist and got some pills, but as far as I can tell, they haven't helped. Ya know, Doc, she even talks about going to college. She's thirty-eight for god's sake and has everything her little heart desires. Now she wants to go to college and even study your trade—psychology. I don't know what the hell that's all about."

I have always prided myself in being able to make contact with my clients, but I found it impossible to feel any warmth or connection with Howard. He talked about Cecelia like she was his maid and the children like nuisances that belonged to someone else.

After about twenty minutes, Cecelia drove up in a Lexus and joined us. Howard didn't get up, but did say, "Hi honey, how's your day been? The Doc here has been asking me why I thought you wanted me to join you here." He turned to me, "Hey, Doc, is this supposed to be marriage counseling?"

Before I could respond, Cecelia said, "Of course it is, Howard. We need to do something to change the way we're living. I'm miserable … honey."

I noticed how difficult it was for her to call him "honey" but Howard didn't seem to catch that.

Howard responded like he really didn't know what she was talking about. "Aw, come on, sweetheart, how could you be miserable? You've got everything you've asked for and the kids are all doing fine and have everything they need. What the hell's the problem? I mean really?" He was working hard to sound reasonable and understanding while he covered up an urge to explode.

Cecelia glanced at me and I nodded; hoping she would see I had her back if she stood up to Mr. Tycoon. "Yes, we have everything, but I feel like one of the Stepford wives and the kids are scared as hell of you. Don't you notice that the kids always come to me for everything?"

"Of course, I notice—you're the mother and mothers are good at taking care of kids. That's their job, right? And what's this Stepford wives shit?

After several minutes trying to explain why they needed to change things in the marriage and family, Cecelia got bolder and said, "Howard, you are so controlling. I and the kids feel like we are prisoners."

With this Howard exploded, "I work my goddamned ass off, giving you guys everything and you're afraid of me? What the hell do you want?" Again, he turned to me, "What's she talking about Doc?"

I told him that he was in the same predicament as many men in our culture. I added, "Cecelia and the kids just want to get to know you—to feel your heart." I was sure someone had taken a chunk out of his heart earlier in life—and it wasn't Cecelia. She was ten years his junior.

"Know my heart? My ass. They just want my wallet." Cecelia shook her head but he went on, "How about this? I'll just leave all of you—I'll set you free and see how you do. I'll find someone who appreciates me and all that I can do for them." He got up and headed for the door. He turned, "And I'll see that all of you are left without a penny! Not one goddamned cent! Hear me?" He slammed the door as he left.

Cecelia was crying and I kept quiet. After a while, she said, "I'm not really crying because of his leaving. I think I'm crying because of what it could have been. You know, I feel sorry for him. The other day, you said that we all need to be strong enough to be gentle. You were referring to being parents. It fits for husbands, too, don't you think?"

"Yes, and you, I think, have found your strength—strength enough to be honest." I knew that Howard was right in one case—Cecelia would have to take a chunk out his wallet. California is a community property state but she would have to fight for every nickel. Howard is a hard man to feel sorry for, let alone feel compassion. I felt a bit sad that I had not been able to reach him. I wondered if it might have helped if I had told him that he, like many men, had been scripted to just be a good provider and little else. He was not a "bad" man but he was very out-of-touch with himself—and far from being strong enough to be gentle. Just as many men need to be gentle, many women, like Cecelia, need to be strong. Of course, both need both strength and gentleness.

Social And Economic Sources Of Violence

I could not live with myself if I did not acknowledge how our history and culture often is a cause of violence. In our society, money, too often, does dominate our lives. Just as Howard attempted to control his family with money, some corporate leaders, institution presidents and others work to control the lives of all of their employees by paying unjustly low wages, threats of being fired, demotions and other tactics. Some CEOs do work to bring justice and sensitivity into their companies and are "strong enough to be gentle"—and kind and just. Too many do not. Injustice itself is a form of violence. Business and agency leaders also need to learn healthier ways to live with themselves—and, I'm sure, enjoy life more.

Unfortunately nearly all cultures put too much emphasis on controlling and having power over others. A truly strong person works to have *power with* and not *power over* other people. There is an increasingly high number of leaders who are realizing this and that bodes well for our future. Fair, gentle, strong and *power-with* leaders have happier and more productive workers. Leaders who inspire their associates and workers prosper far more than those who use power over tactics like threats and abuse. I'm sure they are able to "live with themselves and enjoy it."

Families, neighborhoods, and the media need to work on this also. When a person grows up in an environment where he or she is constantly encouraged to "kick ass" whenever they feel threatened or disrespected in some way, it is not surprising that he or she finds it hard to understand what we mean when we say, "Be strong enough to be gentle." All we can do is work on ourselves and present examples like Jesus, Ghandi, Mandela, Martin Luther King, and others. I consider myself a non-violent person but I am not sure I would have been able to keep that stance if members of my own family were being directly threatened. I do know, however, that I have often been able to solve conflicts with diplomacy and in a non-violent manner.

There is a difference between being passive and being non-violent. What a wonderful world we would have if all national leaders believed and effectively worked to promote gentle power-sharing between all people and all countries. Teachers, news people, and parents are also leaders and need to help create a more gentle and peaceful world by not perpetuating fear. Violence most often, has as its source fear. It takes a strong person to face his or her own fear and be non-violent in handling threats and direct violence. A wonderful world would also be a peaceful world—and war would become obsolete. I just thought of a great poster I saw during the Vietnam War—*What If They Gave A War and Nobody Came?*

It is a social kind of violence when a large percentage of the population is starving.

And it is a form of violence when a country spends billions of dollars on armaments and cannot afford to pay teachers and other staff a professional and living wage. Having a strong and gentle attitude toward our society and businesses demands that we continue to work on understanding others—the topic of the next chapter.

Chapter 7

LEARNING TO UNDERSTAND

I have found it to be of enormous value when I can permit myself to understand another person.

Carl Rogers

Once a human being has arrived on this earth, communication is the largest single factor determining what kind of relationship she or he makes with others and what happens to each in the world.

Virginia Satir

BEFORE UNDERSTANDING WE NEED TO TRUST

Being the second youngest in a family of eight children, I learned early to keep my thoughts and ideas to myself. If I said out loud what I was thinking, most often I would get teased or laughed at for being ignorant or stupid. When I was twelve years old, I announced to my family that I was going to go to college when I finished high school. The response I got was, "Who the hell do you think you are?" I did go to college and collected five degrees. But it took me well into adulthood to trust anyone with my inner thoughts and questions. Of course, this meant that I was lonely because I had isolated myself. Fortunately for me, I did learn to occupy myself with other things like reading, studying others, gardening, and woodworking.

I liked to think of myself as "the strong, silent type." I doubt the "strong," but I definitely had a silent type in my script. Men, historically, have been scripted to be hunters, providers and protectors, not "trusters" nor "understanders" So, I, and boys and men generally, need to learn how to trust others whereas women have been scripted to be "people persons." While men were out hunting or fighting, women were back with the clan relating with one another and with the children. Most women have a much easier way of understanding others' emotions and frailties than men—it is like it is built into their DNA. A man might say, "Oh, I know Joe, he runs the machine shop down on Main Street—does good work, I like him." He would be surprised to learn from his wife that he and his wife were getting a divorce because he abused their children and was unkind to his wife and nearly everyone else in his family.

LEARNING TO TRUST

Which comes first, trusting or being trustworthy? I believe they come together. A good place to start is to share a 'small' inner thought or secret. I call it sending out a "trial balloon" and see how it flies. One time, when I was in college and working many hours during the summer vacation, one of my older brothers invited me to visit him and his family in California.

Just before boarding the train in Kansas, I got a bright idea about how I might begin to overcome my social isolation. I decided to sit by as many people as possible. First, I would see if a person I sat beside would begin a conversation with me in three minutes. If they did not, then I would try to start a conversation with them and see if they would oblige. I sat by twenty-six people (Yes, I kept count) on that train ride and only one nice, gray-haired lady started talking to me before the end of three minutes. Only one young man in a Navy uniform would not respond when I tried to start a discussion. All of the other twenty-four people and I had short to long conversations about many things. Some told me a great deal about their families, professions, hopes and dreams. Others didn't get much beyond the weather. In the dining car at breakfast, there was only one vacant chair. It was at a table for two and a very pretty young woman was sitting at the table. Now that was a challenge for me. A little voice inside me said, "Well, Don, are you a coward or do you have enough courage to ask if you could sit with her?" I took a deep breath and, with the kind of courage it would take to jump off of the thirty foot diving board, I approached the table and put my hand on the chair. I courageously asked, "Ah, um, ah, may I sit here?" Surprisingly, she said, "Yes." I think I could have fallen in love, except she was going to California to enter the convent.

All in all, it was a delightful beginning of my coming out of my social shell. I learned that most people are reactive, rather than proactive. I continued to experiment with that idea, and I have become quite adept at trusting others and being delighted by them. I worked, also, to develop my sense of discernment and rarely opened up to gossips or to those who seemed shallow to me. I think it is good to be open and discerning—they are not contradictory.

BEING TRUSTWORTHY AND UNDERSTANDING

After years of listening to people and sometimes hurting others by revealing something that I should have kept confidential, I have become increasingly trustworthy. Many people have told me that they felt free to tell me anything. That feels very good to me and I have been able to make connections with many wonderful people.

Truly understanding another person is one of the most difficult, and rewarding tasks in life. It is also one that is easily missed. After spending time with another human, child or adult, man or woman, we often think that we have gotten to know them and understand them—and usually we have only scratched the surface. I would like to share a poem written by a friend of mine, Howard Miller, who makes the point clearly and poetically:

THE PAIN OF VINCENT VAN SCHMO

I paint pictures of the people in my life
And then look at those paintings
INSTEAD OF THEM
I hate Disappointment....
Especially when people deviate
From my expectations
Which causes me
At times....
Awful disappointments
While my paintings are consistent
In that I get what I paint....
I am usually happy with my paintings
Of others....
But....
The pictures I paint of myself
Even though I create them
Are my biggest Disappointment
I guess I am just not
A very good Artist....
But I will keep trying
Until....
I run out of paint.

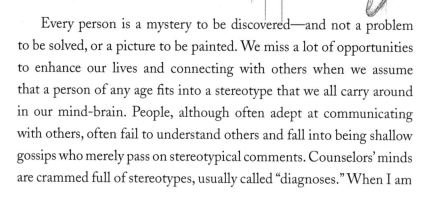

Every person is a mystery to be discovered—and not a problem to be solved, or a picture to be painted. We miss a lot of opportunities to enhance our lives and connecting with others when we assume that a person of any age fits into a stereotype that we all carry around in our mind-brain. People, although often adept at communicating with others, often fail to understand others and fall into being shallow gossips who merely pass on stereotypical comments. Counselors' minds are crammed full of stereotypes, usually called "diagnoses." When I am working with a counseling intern, I tell them I do not want to know the diagnosis of a client. I want to hear their story. A diagnosis is too inclusive a "story" and makes, say a person who is depressed, sound like all other persons who are depressed. Each person's condition is their individual story.

Never fall into the habit of seeing understanding as simple or complete. Or say such things as "I see right through him." "I can read her like a book." "He is so simple-minded." These comments are never true. We humans are very complex beings—even the so-called "simple minded" ones. Listening is an art in itself. It usually takes hours of *active listening* to truly understand another person. Active listing entails feeding back to the speaker what we understand him or her to be saying. Too often, we say we understand when we only have a small clue.

Trust, Understanding, And The I-Thou Concept

Carl Rogers was one of the most influential psychologists of our time and was a master of understanding. One person who contributed to Roger's thinking was Martin Buber. As a young professor, Martin Buber was required to be available to troubled students. In his book, *I-Thou,* he tells of a tragic incident that inspired his life's work. A young man, around twenty, came to see him. I will call the student Mark. Mark was very depressed but disguised it with just talking about the difficulties he had with college life—living in a dormitory, being away from his family, and many other things that nearly all students experience. Three hours after Mark left, another student rushed into Buber's office and announced that Mark had hanged himself.

He was dead.

Buber spent many hours pondering the one hour he had spent with Mark. Buber thought he had listened respectfully to the boy.

He had not been judgmental, belittling, or unkind. He had taken his concerns seriously but, obviously, too lightly. All in all, the young professor decided he had been a reasonably good counselor to Mark. He knew that possibly there was nothing he could have said that would have prevented his death, but he continued to be haunted by his suicide. After several days, it dawned on Buber that one of the biggest mistakes he had made was this: He left Mark in the role of student and counselee, and Martin Buber left himself in the role of professor-counselor. He did not give himself permission or time to truly understand the student by going deeper into what was troubling him. He allowed himself to be satisfied with superficial ideas and did not truly open himself, as a person, to the fellow.

It was a role-to-role meeting, not a person-to-person meeting. Martin continued to work on what he considered his most important discovery, and what became a major contribution to counseling and psychotherapy—the *I-Thou Concept*. Just as I, the speaker and/or observer, am an individual who has a unique history and sense of self, you, the *Thou*, and the person I am talking to and relating with, is a unique man or woman with a special history and sense of self. You are not an "It" or a robotic being performing the task of talking to me. I wish I had known this when I was six years old and my dad called me a worthless piece of shit. That was the worst "it" I have ever personally encountered.

Martin Buber realized he had hidden behind the "professor mask." Even professional counselors need to guard against putting on a mask that leads to an I-It relationship when working with the person who is his or her client or patient. Recently a young woman came to me for counseling. She had gone to a clinic recommended by her insurance. She saw a psychiatrist for fifteen minutes and then was turned over to a nurse-practitioner. The nurse looked at the psychiatrist's notes and said to the young woman, "Well, it looks like you may be bi-polar, have a schizo-affective disorder, and are depressed."

The young woman had gone into the clinic feeling a bit anxious and came out with extreme anxiety. The two counselors did not take the time to get to know her at all—to them, she was an *IT*—a typical young woman who had some problems. No one is typical anything.

A person is putting on a mask when he or she is trying to make a good impression, or close a "deal", or just to avoid making contact in a way that would reveal who they really are. It is important to realize that the real person behind the mask is far more complex and interesting.

Virginia Satir states in her book, *Peoplemaking*, that nearly all of us think it is necessary to hide our true selves behind some kind of mask or defense. By the time we are six years old, we have had thousands of communication experiences and we have developed hundreds of impressions. Examples: We may have known only one elderly person and that was a grouchy grandfather, so when we see or meet a gray-haired person, we assume they are unfriendly. If we have grown up in a hard-working but poor family and meet a doctor or professor, we may assume that he or she came from a wealthy family and never experienced any kind of poverty. I grew up in such a family and I was sure every professional person could not be interested in me in any way. A fat person, we may assume, lacks self-discipline. A shy pretty young woman is stuck-up. I could go on and on. I hope you get the idea. Even well-educated, professional people often have this tendency. In our twenty-first century, too many health professionals treat people as though they were lab rats—and not *Thous*.

EVEN MARRIED COUPLES NEED TO BE *I-THOU*

George and Christine had been married for twenty-two years and came to see me for marriage counseling. Both were in their early forties and both professionals who were doing well in their respective fields. They were having a hard time communicating and what was unusual, the wife was the least understanding of the two. Christine continually called George, "my husband," and never just "George" even when he was sitting next to her. It seemed like a small thing but after a few sessions, I realized that this symbolized one of the problems between them. Christine was not a shallow person but had come from a family that seemed to be. She had picked up a way of communicating that kept her and her husband apart. They had what Buber calls an *I-It* relationship—a role-to-role partnership.

It has been amazing to me how many couples continue for years in an I-It relationship. It is not a Joe-Susan relationship, it is a husband-wife relationship, or an I-It, or role-role relationship. In a marriage, the I/It couple have very clear ideas about what each partner should do and be. The wife is the homemaker and caretaker of the children (she may also work outside the home but that is secondary), the husband works, pays the bills, and probably does the yard work. Any deviation from this is considered bad or wrong.

WE UNDERSTAND OURSELVES AS WE UNDERSTAND OTHERS

If you have learned to practice some of the steps already suggested— then, you are well on your way to understanding yourself. This prepares you for the step of more deeply listening to another person—and to be a trusting person who is able to share your experiences with him or her.

There are some relationships in which a friend or "superior," a boss, supervisor, or partner who believes that the only way to trust someone is to know all about him or her. What they are looking for is someone who thinks exactly like they do and promises to never deviate from their past way of thinking and doing things. "I trust you because I know what you think and what you will do in every situation." That is not trust, it is a kind of mental slavery. One of the things I least liked when I was a priest was that I was treated as a role—a minister—1 and not as me, a unique person. I should have known better because the ordination ceremony has a line that went something like this, "You no longer live, but Christ lives through you." At the time, I thought it was just symbolic. The New Testament has a line something like this and it means that a person is putting away his "false" or immature self and devoting himself to a more mature and ideal way of being. A similar kind of misunderstanding of the I/Thou, and of intimacy happens when a wife, or husband, who says of her or his partner, "I trust him because I know exactly what he is doing every moment of the day." Is this trust or an invisible leash?

To truly understand another person, it is very helpful for us to deeply understand ourselves. Native American shamans say that we need to be enchanted with our own stories to be healthy. One of my therapy mentors, after hearing me tell of an incident in my life, said, "Don, tell us that story again. You sound like you're reading a telephone book. That was a dramatic moment in your life. Put some drama in the telling." I tried several times but couldn't get into the excitement, or enchantment, that the story deserved. It was only later that I realized I had never appreciated the wonder of my own life. I then began to take a new and more accepting view of my life story. At the same time, I began to be more interested and enchanted with others' experiences and life stories.

That same mentor, Erv Polster, wrote *Every Person's Life is Worth a Novel*. As I mentioned earlier, I would change it to *Every Person's Life is Worth Several Novels*. Or, as a friend suggested, every person's life is worth a novel, a play, two short stories, several limericks, and a eulogy. We humans are very complex and enchanted beings.

Start with spending some time observing an infant or toddler; if they do not fascinate you, please find someone who will inject some life into you. You and I were there once and because we received at least a minimum amount of nurturing and understanding, we are alive today. And we are wonder-full and lovable beings—the topic of the next chapter.

Chapter 8

BEING A LOVING PERSON

No matter what great things a man may do in life, unless he becomes a loving person, his life is a failure.

Don Hanley, 1964

God is love, and he who lives in love, lives in God, and God in him.

John's Letters,
New Testament

ON BEING A LOVING PERSON

When I was growing up, I never heard the word "love" aside from love songs on the radio and in movies. No one in the family ever said, "I love you," at least that I heard. Around the time I went to the seminary, I thought about how unhappy my parents were, along with my four married brothers and two married sisters. So marriage was not a road to happiness or love, and that was one of the reason I wanted to become a priest—so I could love everyone and be close to no one. It was only after ordination and Anne telling me, "I love you," that I realized that was not possible. Before that momentous event, I limited love to just being kind and charitable.

I originally entitled this chapter, "On Becoming a Loving Person." Now I believe we are born as loving beings and our challenge is to learn to develop that human power or inheritance that is within us. I think that this is such a difficult task, especially for men and many women, that we give up or, like me, find it so incredibly difficult that, for those close to us, it becomes a life-long task. At age 82, I'm still working on it—especially with those closest to me—Anne, our two daughters, and our three grandchildren.

LOVE STRONGER THAN FEAR

When I speak of love, I mean a power that is stronger than fear. I mean a kind of energy that breathes meaning into life. It is an energy that defies nature's tendency to diminish and destroy life, but causes us to grow and flourish in every way. It is the triumph of the human spirit that allows us to overcome the distances between us and other persons brought on by our selfish tendencies. True love even triumphs over death.

We inherit the ability to love but often are scripted by family, schooling, and ironically, religion, to lose that ability. Many contemporary spiritual writers and positive psychologists contend that we humans are *naturally loving beings.* They write that we are born to connect to others and to be compassionate. The above quote from St. John's Epistle stating that God is love, were the words that kept me in the seminary. I remember very much disliking the dogmas and moralisms of my religion, but felt hopeful when I read scripture passages such as this. They also kept me in the priesthood for six years.

Just as we have not been educated to make choices early in life, but not educated to accept ourselves, so we have not been educated to develop our power to love. And we are never too old to learn—or refine it. Many people ask, "If we are naturally loving and compassionate, why is there so much child abuse, so many rapes, murders, assaults, and wars?" First of all, we are part of a system that is finite and breakable and that means our mind-brains are vulnerable and easily led astray. Fear and the need for safety and security often seem more important than loving. Also, I believe that a big part of the problem is that we are, formally and informally, educated to think that we are not positively wonderful and loving beings. I often wonder if many people in power—political, military, police, religious, and education leaders— want to keep people ignorant so they can remain in positions of power.

GROWING AND EVOLVING INTO LOVING PERSONS

Another reason we are not always loving and compassionate is that we are all evolving beings. Just as the earth, with all of its inhabitants, is evolving, so each of us humans, late-comers on earth (only three million years) continue to evolve. Perhaps, I should say, *should* evolve, because some people seem to live and act like undisciplined young children, even into old age. Of course, if you are reading this, you are not one of them. Right?

There are many people who have been so traumatized as small children that it seems impossible to become loving persons. And some children seem to be born without a conscience—the sociopaths. I actually heard a man, after being asked whether or not his wife loved him, say, "By god, she better, of I'll beat the shit out of her." Unfortunately, he wasn't joking. Likewise on the other extreme, there are people who were so coddled, protected, and pampered that they never struggled for anything and thus stay rather spoiled, selfish adults who believe their purpose in life is to be taken care of by others and to gain power over as many people as possible. Meeting the challenge of loving and growing is definitely part of becoming truly loving persons.

I read of a species of great apes in Africa called *bonobos*. They are cousins of chimpanzees, and unlike the chimps, are very non-violent. Like humans, their sexuality is more than just procreation; it is a way of bonding. Matriarchs gently rule the groups. Some paleontologists and anthropologists suggest that humans are descended from the chimps and not bonobos. If so, that is too bad—for us. Ninety-some percent of the DNA of both bonobos and chimps match ours. If we could connect more with our bonobo DNA maybe we wouldn't have to struggle so long to become truly loving persons.

Also on human evolution: A scientist and spiritual writer, Teilhard de Chardin, believes that the next step in human evolution is the "amorization" of humans. My spell-checker corrected "amorization" to become "amortization." The spelling experts, I guess, better reflect our society that seems to put money above loving. Teilhard was French and he meant the spiritual community of humans in love or "amore" as the future we are striving for. A wonderful idea and, of course, it cannot be proven. Our far distant descendants will know— I hope. In the meantime it is a great philosophy—far superior to the gloom and doom of so many.

The other day I saw a delightful cartoon that showed a boy about eight years old standing in front of his class and holding the hand of an old man (who kind of looked like me). The boy said, "This my grandpa. He is going to tell us why our country is going to hell in a hand-basket." Honestly, I don't think that is so; we will never find a utopia, but we can, hopefully, help create a more pleasant world.

It is an important evolutionary fact is that males and females have evolved very differently. As mentioned earlier, ninety-plus percent of our time on earth has been as hunters and gatherers. Men were away from their families and clan, often for long periods, while the women remained with the other women, the children, elderly, and disabled males. Therefore women developed relational, nurturing, and bonding skills that men did not.

During this evolution, many researchers believe the brains of men and women have changed. The connection between the left hemisphere and right hemisphere of the brain, called the *corpus coliseum*, differ. In women, it is like a super-highway, and in men, a one lane road. This is the reason women are often multi-taskers; they can fix a meal while taking care of a baby, talking on the phone, doing the dishes, and reading the paper. Whereas I'll say, "Everybody clear out of the kitchen and hold my calls; I'm making a sandwich."

Teilhard's dream of a world-wide loving community of men and women means that men and women must learn to love deeply and for longer periods of time as we increasingly live longer. We will experience the love and bonding differently and hopefully respect that difference.

MALE AND FEMALE EXPRESSIONS OF LOVE AND COMPASSION

I like this quote from Maya Angelou:

> *I dared to love. By love I mean that condition in the human spirit so profound, it encourages us to develop courage and build bridges in attempts to reach other human beings, and then to trust those bridges and cross those bridges in attempts to reach other human beings."*

Maya expresses deep thoughts and adds passion. It is an example of reason and emotion.

Here is another, written by a friend, Russ Shor, in his unpublished manuscript: The woman has been betrayed by her lover and she says:

Maybe you think I'm just a plain shop girl you could take advantage of, but look—really look—at me. I have feelings, I cry, I laugh, I … I love Christmas cards and Easter eggs. Can you feel … understand? My heart can dance, soar, hope and break. I'm happy when a customer thanks me and smiles. I'm all of those things. And I love. I have love. It was all for you … I gave myself to you … I did that for no other man. Only you!

I think this is a beautiful expression of feelings and love and I can't imagine myself spontaneously saying these words. And I cannot imagine any man I know doing so. Many men would just dismiss it as just a woman's rant. In Shor's writing, the poor man simply says, "I'm sorry."

The women's big *corpus coliseum* that connects her left and right brain allows her to express her thoughts AND feelings in a much fuller way than men. Women cannot have a thought without an accompanying feeling. Many times, over the years, I have worked with a man in therapy and found the man very articulate both about his thoughts and his feelings. Then when his wife joins us, he seems tongue-tied and defers to her in our discussions. I believe it is because she is used to easily expressing both her feelings and thoughts at the same time, and he is not. Still, men and women need to pursue working on understanding each other and to accept that they see things differently. Love between a man and woman is, of course, a necessary and wonderful challenge and adventure. And it is a more difficult challenge than climbing the Matterhorn.

As stated at the beginning of this chapter, the Christian Bible's New Testament (John I) states, "God is love, and he who lives in love, lives in God and God in him." All major religions state that love is the basis for all of life and God's challenge to everyone. And then the religion's adherents start fighting over who has the best god and the best message, set of rules, and best path to reaching that god—and completely forgetting the original message of love. Christians say, "Love thy neighbor as you love yourself." And we have been doing exactly that for 2,000 years—we've never learned to love ourselves and so we go to war. That is an inheritance we can do without. Religious intolerance need not turn us off to pursuing love and teaching our children to love—hopefully by our example.

Thomas Merton, a monk and spiritual writer, suggests that we can spend our entire lifetime climbing the ladder of success and then when we reach the top, find that the ladder is against the wrong wall. Climbing the ladder of love is always against the right wall, and only that wall will lead us to know how wonder-full we are. And then, we will live with our selves and enjoy it!

Chapter 9

BEING CREATIVE AND JOYFUL

The world was left unfinished so that humans could have a part in creation.

Rabbi Irwin Kula

You can never really lose your soul; you can only fail to realize it.

Joseph D. Dillon

ON THE NEED TO BE CREATIVE

Even six-year-olds can live with themselves and enjoy it—and be creative. One of my favorite stories is the one about the first-grade teacher who saw her little student drawing furiously. The teacher asks, "What are you drawing, Debbie?"

"A picture of God."

"But Debbie, Honey, nobody knows what God looks like."

Debbie: "They will in a minute!"

I believe that Debbie was closer to "seeing" God than most of the popular religious preachers. She is like the four-year-old who asks his baby sister to tell him about God. I say we all know what God looks like—if we know how to look. God manifests Himself in

the world we live in—in the sun, the sky, the trees, the flowers, the animals, and most especially in our own hearts and in the hearts of all other human beings. God is with and in us. I truly believe this. We have the power to help create and shape our world and this, hopefully, is a delightful and joyful task. I wish my early religious education had taught me this instead of teaching me what a miserable sinner I was.

If you are one of those fortunate few who work in a field that is creative and allows you to follow your bliss, then thank your creative self, your parents, mentors, friends, and The Force that is with you. Unfortunately, too many people on this planet are unable to even think about what their bliss might be. They are too busy trying to feed, shelter and clothe their families, each and every day. If you are reading these words, you are among the minority on earth who knows how to read and has the leisure time to pick up a book or an e-book. I hope it is a creative and enjoyable endeavor for you—and that you are learning, being motivated, joyfully to be engaged in some life-giving pursuit.

Unfortunately, learning to choose, to accept ourselves, to love, and be joyfully creative is not encouraged in our culture—nor in most other "developed" countries. Success, too often, is measured by how much money or prestigious social position a person possesses. In college, I had a textbook in an education course that stated: "The purpose of education is to produce good consumers and producers."

After counseling hundreds of depressed men and women, I saw that as they began to feel more involved in life, their "creative juices" began to flow and they were taking a more joyful interest in other people. It might appear through their employment and if not, it showed up in their leisure time. If it is not the nature of your work to be creative, find a way to make it so. I always thought that being a traffic cop would be a terribly boring job. Then, sometime in the 1990's, I saw a segment of Sixty Minutes that featured a policeman directing traffic in Brooklyn. He was dancing and smiling and greeting everyone who passed through his intersection. After showing several minutes of his delightful routine, a journalist interviewed him. He was a native of Jamaica and had been on the police force for many years and said, "This is the most wonderful job in the world—for me."

Dr. Maslow's hierarchy of needs, states that the basic or dependency—"D"—needs are the ones I've already mentioned: physical needs, safety and security, love and belonging, self-esteem, and autonomy. We are dependent on these being met on a regular basis to be a healthy person. And when we have them met consistently, we can pursue the "B," or Being needs of Creativity: Beauty, the Arts, and Self-Actualization. We have mistakenly thought that our self-esteem was based on how "successful" we are in gaining prestige and/or material goods. John and Jane Doe are successful because they have a Cadillac and Bentley and live in a million dollar house. We too often believe that is the way to gain high self-esteem; and at the same time, we know that it is not.

I just watched a brief video about an experienced bicycle rider who took eight months to learn how to ride a bike that had a handle bar that turned right when the wheel turned left. He was experimenting with how rigid our mind-brains are when we learn one way to do something and then find changing what we have learned to be very difficult. His three-year old son, who had just learned how to ride a regular bike, learned the new "wrong-way" bike in three weeks. So if we want to learn to really enjoy ourselves and how we live, we will have to learn some new ways of thinking about ourselves and our life. Hopefully, we have had some experience doing that when we were younger.

OVERCOMING HABITS AND MOODS TO BE CREATIVE

Most of us have grown up thinking of Native Americans as uneducated and uncultured because many of them did not have a written language. It has taken us centuries to realize that they had a rich culture and profound spiritual lives. Below is, for me, a powerful example:

Native American Shamans, according to anthropologist Angeles Arrien, often used a wonderful set of questions when encountering a man or woman who seemed lethargic, stuck, or perhaps, depressed. These questions, I believe are superior to many currently used by psychotherapists. They are:

1. When did you stop singing?

    The shamans were probably thinking of joining in tribal rituals or celebrations. I am suggesting that we sing out loud whenever we wish, even if we have a hard time carrying a note. Take some time to memorize a catchy tune that you find enjoyable. When I lost my job as a graduate school president and all the money we had put in the school, I was very depressed. One of my daughters suggested I take a singing class. I did and it was very therapeutic. I think I even sang better afterwards—in the shower.

2. When did you stop dancing?

    When you are dancing, you are in touch with your four bones:

    a. Your backbone—for courage: Courage to give hugs, initiate conversations, stand up to people who are pushing you or someone whom you need to help..

    b. Your wishbone—to develop your hopes and dreams.

    c. Your funny bone—for humor: To laugh at yourself is a sign of maturity and to just plain laugh when you encounter something humorous.

    d. Your hollow bone—for being open to the divine or the universe. This helps us gain a certain openness to power beyond ourselves, and to connect with others and with the universe.

3. When did you stop being enchanted with stories—especially your own?

As I mentioned in Chapter 4, we need to tell our stories to understand ourselves and even to give ourselves appreciation for surviving difficult situations. To appreciate our history or just to acknowledge it, is to appreciate and acknowledge ourselves.

4. When did you stop being comfortable with silence?
Sometimes it is helpful to think of a bout of depression as a time to retreat and to contemplate our life and our possible creative endeavors we may undertake. Think of being depressed as shutting down or shutting off our creative energy. We need to take time to open our own creative valve.

If you are practicing all of these, then you are open to joy and creativity. Please note, drugs and alcohol *shut off* our creative juices except in rare instances when the drinking helps us to lose some inhibitions and introduces us to our own love of dancing or some other creative and joyous activity. If we continue to rely on drinking to enjoy the activity, we lose both our joy and creativity. I also believe that we abandon our creative center when we use our genius only to make more money or become better thieves or manipulators of other people. If our creative endeavors hurt the environment or is life-destroying in any way, it will be a destructive force. There is no creativity in this pursuit.

General George Custer (in)famously said, "The only good Indian is a dead Indian." I wonder if he ever took the time to get to know any of them and learned of their practices and beliefs. I recently ran across an enlightening book entitled, *The Spiritual Journey of a Brave Heart* by Basil Brave Heart, a Lakota Native-American. Brave Heart noted, "In my growing up years, it was part of our life to make prayer when the sun was just going down. Whenever something ends, something begins. So there is no death. It's just a transformation." If Custer had taken time to get to know the Lakotas, he would not have made such horrible statements. So make your creations life-giving.

LEARNING FROM CHILDREN

I learned a great deal about being creative from our daughters when they were quite young. When our youngest, Micaela, was around four years old, she liked playing with her "little people." The people were two inches high and looked a lot like the present little people in South Park. One time, she began to assemble the small folks and all their accouterments— fences, houses, pets, etc.— into a makeshift village in our screened-in porch. This project took her several weeks and we were instructed not to touch it or step on any of the people. One day, I hid behind a door and listened to her as she was assembling the village. Each "person" had a first and last time and they "talked" to one another. As I listened to her, I realized she was creating a novel or soap opera. I don't remember how many weeks this went on, but it was definitely a part time creative adventure she was devoted to. At the end, she pushed all her "creatures" into a pile and put them into the toy box. She stood up, shrugged her shoulders and sighed, as if to say, "All done." She now has a Masters in Fine Arts and is editor of a magazine.

As far back as I can remember, I was always taught not to "waste time," and to have a practical purpose for everything I did. Even today, I need to have a practical reason for everything I do. For example, I enjoy writing and I must give myself an excuse to do so. Maybe I'll get something published and make some money and leave some kind of positive legacy for posterity. This is baloney; I should write because I enjoy it and it gets my creative juices flowing. Oh, that's a practical idea, too—but an okay one.

CREATIVE ART HELPS MATH AND SCIENCE

One of my irritants is that the arts—art, music, dance, acting, creative writing—are the first things that get dropped in the schools when the budget gets tight. If we want to raise happy, productive and creative people, they should be the most important courses offered. I have heard of elementary schools that have cancelled recess! That has to be one of the most wrong-headed things I have ever heard of. If the students are happy and enjoying learning, they will also find a way to do the "practical" things like math and science. A wonderful program in Venezuela teaches poor children to play a musical instrument. The music is classical and many of the children learn to make their own violins, cellos, drums, and more. Hundreds have graduated from the programs—like Gustav Dudamel, director of the Los Angeles Philharmonic Orchestra. A far larger proportion of the Venezuelan students complete elementary and secondary school than those who do not participate in the program.

Sometimes, we need to make a decision to bring art or music into our lives. I have two friends in their sixties who have done exactly that. One has taken nearly every art course, and there are many, that the local community college offers. The other one is learning to play the guitar that he has wanted to do since he was a teen.

Just think of the creative things you can be doing: gardening, wood working, learning a new song, writing, dancing, hiking, and traveling—even if only through Google Earth, getting to know more people, helping out at a local food kitchen or food bank, visiting the sick and elderly who can't read or walk.

As I was writing this, I realized that I was never bored as a child and teenager; I had too many things to do. I realize, looking back, that I was being creative when I won a poster contest when I was eleven years old, built several pieces of furniture in wood-working class, and when I built a two-bedroom house when I was twenty-one. "Look, Mom, at what I did all by myself." At the time, I just thought of it as something I did because I needed to leave something that would help Mom have some income. I have to admit that I was more than a little disappointed when Mom only said, "That's nice, son."

We must grow older, but we don't need to become grouchy old curmudgeons. Once when Anne and I were eating in a restaurant, two elderly couples came in and passed our table. The two women looked quite alive and interesting but the two men had sour and grumpy looks on their faces. I muttered to Anne. "When I begin looking like that, please shoot me." She responded, "I'm not going to jail for you." She's so selfish.

The majority of us here in the United States enjoy a life-style that is the envy of much of the world. Why then, do we spend so much time, money and energy on being distracted from that life? Some of these things are creative for the inventors, engineers, and craftsmen, but not for the people who use them. Massive roller-coasters that scare us nearly to death, are true wonders of the world, but I wish all that money and energy had gone into creating water and sewage systems for the people of the world. I am amazed at the creativity of those who make horror movies that rake in hundreds of millions of dollars, video war games, and many other things that do nothing more than allow us to escape from being more creative ourselves. Too many children grow up with gadgets that occupy their time and keep them busy, but only a few become creative makers of entertainment for others. And adults in the U.S. spend 91 BILLION dollars a year on gambling. Is this a creative endeavor?

So, let's get our own creative juices flowing! We can be co-creators of our world.

Chapter 10

FAILING, FALLING AND GETTNG UP

God, grant me the serenity to accept the things I cannot change, the courage to change things I can change and the wisdom to know the difference.

Reinhold Niebur

For those who understand, no explanation is necessary. For those who do not understand, none will suffice.

Anonymous

ON FINDING SERENITY AND WISDOM

I have always had difficulty in finding serenity in accepting things I cannot change—especially those things which I do not like—in myself and in the world. When I was a young child, of course, I did not serenely accept being called stupid, clumsy, ugly and all that. Now as I recall those years I do not feel serene but I can accept that that is part of my history. Now at the age of 82, I am working toward feeling serene about being an old man whose get-up-and-go has almost gotten up and gone. Maybe accepting it and laughing about it at times is being serene.

If whatever is happening around me, like the weather, that I can do nothing about, it is important to just accept it and continue breathing and realize that this will not go on forever. If I begin to complain about everything I cannot change, I just become an old grouch and someone no one wants to be around. Over the years, it has been interesting to find so many people who are just plain unpleasant come to therapy and complain about everyone and everything and then wonder why they are so depressed. One of the first things I ask people when they begin therapy is: "Who are your support people in your life?" Too often, they respond that they do not have any. A recent trend is for a young client to say they have many friends on Facebook or some other social network. The latter are usually not sufficient to be the kind of support that is needed.

We have the ability to be serene in difficult situations if we stay in touch with our own power. Many years ago, I was president of a graduate school and I and the school were being sued by a fellow in another city. His attorney court-ordered me to give a deposition on the issues involved. Fortunately for me, I was taking a yoga class at the time. Not wanting to pay for an attorney to go with me, I made the journey alone. My plan was to relax my body and be in touch with my breathing. I expected to confront an attorney who would shout questions at me. That is exactly what I encountered. So I sat at a long conference table with only a court reporter, my accuser, and his attorney present. I sat as relaxed as possible. Every time the lawyer loudly asked a question or accused me of something, I took a deep breath, felt my feet on the floor, and quietly and thoughtfully responded. This went on for three hours and when I got in my car, I felt more relaxed than when I arrived. The only mar to my serenity was my rather joyful feeling that those two guys were up-the-wall and angry as little wet hens. I could not change them, but I could change myself and find peace and strength in myself. My attorney pretended to be hurt when, after reading the transcript, said, "I guess you don't need me anymore." I have used my own example many times since then.

Usually, when we take a moment to reflect on what is the best way to respond to someone or something, we will tap into our own inner wisdom. For me, wisdom is a combination of research, experience, intuitive knowing, and being in touch with the universal knowledge of humankind—what Carl Jung refers to as *cosmic consciousness*. Of course, this requires relaxation and attentiveness.

On Coping And Learning From Failure

As I look back from the vantage point of eight decades, I realize that many episodes of what I thought were failures turned out to be opportunities for growth. For example, I was crushed to learn I had flunked the first grade when I was seven years old. It turned out to have been a blessing for by the sixth grade, I was considered the smartest kid in the class. Still it took me several decades to own that I was intellectually gifted. Another experience that I had considered a failure was not being accepted into a missionary order to study for the priesthood. As it happened, years later I began to believe that proselytizing or persuading others to believe and practice my religion, is not a creative or life-giving endeavor. Now, I believe that helping people to think for themselves and to be free, creative thinkers is a far more positive thing to do.

Now, I am going to take a risk and assume that you, having read this far, are the kind of person who understands—and thus does not need an explanation. So I will share with you my worst failure—and one I could have changed much earlier in my life, but didn't. I am an alcoholic. At least, that is the way Alcoholics Anonymous would recommend that I say it. I believe it is more accurate to say that for twenty years, I let alcohol take a hold on my life and my thinking that was hurtful to me and those around me, especially my immediate family.

Good judgment comes from experience and many experiences come from bad judgments. I have two older brothers and two older sisters who were functioning alcoholics, so I should have known better after observing how their drinking had hurt their lives and the lives of their family members. For years, I thought I was superior to them in this area of life. In my late teens and early twenties I avoided drinking and when asked what I thought of beer, I responded, "It should be poured back in the horse."

When I was a priest I occasionally would have a beer or three and, especially when I was at the summer program in Chicago, I often had several beers in the evenings and had a good time teaching others to do the Zorba the Greek folk dance. I had a great time and fortunately did not take the beer drinking practice back home with me.

When I was thirty-five, I transferred from the Wichita, Kansas Diocese to the Oklahoma City Diocese. I was first assigned to live at a downtown parish, under the tutelage of an elderly companionable priest who was, in retrospect, a functioning alcoholic. In Wichita, I always had many evening meetings, classes or other obligations and stayed sober when so occupied. Sometimes in open evenings I would have some scotch or wine. In Oklahoma City, my schedule was not full at all and almost every evening, I would sit with the elderly fellow and have two glasses of scotch on-the-rocks, go to dinner and have two glasses of wine, return to the TV room and have one or two glasses of cognac. All three of the beverages were of the best vintage and went down smoothly. When I left that parish after five months, I craved a drink every evening, but never gave a thought that I had become an alcoholic. I often had some kind of hangover but never let myself take off work or miss any kind of assignment. I was not even aware that I was doing what my siblings had done for years—I was a "functioning" alcoholic but denied it.

The worst part of it was that I carried this habit of drinking into my marriage when I left the priesthood. I rarely got "plastered" or "falling-down drunk" but I drank enough almost every free evening that resulted in me being a pain in the ass. I continued to think I only had a minor problem with alcohol and I was just exercising my autonomy by drinking whenever I wished.

My illusion that I had only a minor problem was shattered when one of my daughters read my narration about my drinking and was angry and hurt by my denial. Living in another state, she sent me an angry and courageous email with the detailed truth. For the first seventeen years of her life, she, her sister and mother, were afraid of me whenever I was drinking. Several times I had hit her and her sister and once I hit her mother while drinking. Several times I had driven drunk with all of them in the car. "Dad," she said, "You were an out-of-control alcoholic."

Hearing that from her and knowing that she was not just trying to hurt me—she just is not that kind of person—I was shaken to my core. I had never had such self-loathing before in my life. My dad's death when I was fourteen, and losing the school we had invested a great many hours of dedicated work and money and taking bankruptcy, had sent me into deep depressions, but both of those incidents were out of my control. My daughter's letter pointed directly to my inadequacies and worth as a person. I had never felt lower in my life.

It Is Never Too Late

For days, I felt like a complete failure as a dad, husband, and as a person. It took me a few days to get up enough courage to call our daughter and apologize and a few days more to apologize to Anne. And the apologies seemed much too shallow for all the hurt I had caused them. Both did say that they still loved me, and that felt so very good to me. Of course, I did not deserve it and I knew that real love is not earned anyway, it is a pure gift.

I am so grateful that the wonderful woman I married and wanted to be with for the rest of my life was patient with me most of the time—for twenty years. I managed to earn a decent living and buy a house and provide for my family. The biggest regret in my life is that I hurt them more than I knew or remembered and I wasn't as emotionally available to them as I could, and should, have been. I have to own the fact that I failed, in many ways, as a father and husband. I am glad that I am living long enough to regret it and to make a few amends. I can say that I am an alcoholic and also a responsible person, and a kind person, and many other identities. Being an alcoholic was not, and is not the whole of who I was or am. For ten years I stayed completely sober. The last fifteen years I have allowed myself two glasses of red wine once or twice a week. Over that time I was not careful and did get drunk. I am ashamed of that, also. I feel that I should be respectful of my family members and not drink any alcohol when I am with them.

On Recovering And Rebuilding

In some very important ways, I needed to be brought down—down from my constant intense inner need to prove myself in some way. I had always felt that I had this hollow place somewhere inside of me that I must find a way of filling in order to be a success as a human being. I thought that if I always worked and studied hard, I would find a way. First, it was getting to the seminary, then it was to be a wonderfully worthwhile and holy priest. I remember when I entered the seminary, thinking I should be humble and holy like St. Francis of Assisi, intelligent and learned like St. Thomas Aquinas, and courageous like St. Francis Xavier. In order to be acceptable, I must be somebody else, other than myself. Fortunately, I did drop that notion before the middle of my seminary years, but the hollow place continued being an antagonistic part of my life. I now realize that that hollow place is our nature's way of keeping us aware that we are limited and finite beings and will be fulfilled only by the infinite force of love.

I began to realize that I must own all parts of myself—and all of my personal history. And that included my failures. As I write this I can say that I am still learning to live with myself, but at this moment of confession, I can't say that I enjoy it. I will accept it and learn to enjoy life, no matter what. If I had somehow managed to make that graduate school a roaring financial success, and had continued drinking and pushing myself in the same intense way as I had done all of my life, I'm quite sure I would have died years ago and been a rather miserable pain-in-the-ass—full time rather than just once in a while.

On Forgiving Ourselves

So, I am hopeful that these words help you to begin accepting yourself in all ways. And I hope your process starts much earlier than mine did. If you have had your own set of failures, I hope you are now forgiving yourself and seeing some of them as something positive and others as wake-up calls. And with the new awareness, you are now beginning to utilize your experiences and your own giftedness to accept the challenges of co-creating your own life and the lives of others around you.

You and I are good and bad, gifted and lacking, resourceful and wounded, happy and sad. Please remember all things, including ourselves, are *both-and*, not either-or. Let us encourage ourselves to enjoy our adventurous journey of life.

Epilogue

CREATING JOYFUL GROWING GROUNDS

Keep two pieces of paper in your pockets at all times, one that says, "I am a speck of dust." and the other, "The world was created for me."

Rabbi Bunim of
P'shiskha

In letting go of your shame, guilt, and powerlessness, you do not lose yourself, but fall into your foundational and grounded self.

Richard Rohr

ON THE IMPORTANCE OF ATTITUDE

Now that you have learned how to live with yourself and enjoy it, let's take a look at how we can enjoy creating a more joyful world for others. Remember Albert Einstein's words: "You can't solve a problem with the same consciousness that caused the problem in the first place." One of the most exciting things that has happened in my lifetime is the revolutionary process in our way of thinking, from a focus on absolute truths to the realization that all thinking is in an evolutionary process of change. Two of the most important thinkers contributing to this are Charles Darwin and Albert Einstein. Their wonderful attitudes led them to create ideas that are fascinating and practical for us to emulate.

I was ordained a priest on May 22nd. 1964 and two weeks later I was sent to a parish to help an Assistant Pastor who was only a few years older than me. After a few days of hearing my enthusiastic ideas about working in a parish, he tells me. "Yep, the first year after ordination, you are going to change the world. The second year, you are going to save your parish. On the third year, you're going to save your own soul. And on the fourth year, you'll be happy to see that the lawn is mowed." Unfortunately, he wasn't kidding. I saw him forty years later and he was still a cynic.

Now, fifty-one years later, I still want to help create a better world, and I'm optimistic that we can. We have already begun to do so, with the condemnation of child abuse, by increasing the number of women and minorities appointed to positions of social responsibility, by legalizing gay marriage, by initiating action to restore a more balanced eco-system, and much more.

Each of us is challenged to grow into fully self-actualizing persons who help with the task—no matter how we began *in utero*. Over the last thirty-five years I have taught or supervised individual, marriage, and family therapists. During ten of those years, one of my tasks was to choose faculty for graduate classes in counseling psychology. After several bad choices, I began making sure that the prospective teacher was able to meet me for lunch. I paid attention to how he or she treated the waiter or waitress. If they treated our server disrespectfully in any way, I would not hire them—no matter where they received their degrees because they would treat students the same way. When I chose counseling interns, I look for intelligence, warmth, compassion, intuitiveness, and joy.

So all of the administrators, teachers, counselors, and care-givers in my joyful new world, will have these characteristic virtues. I'll start at the very beginning, a very good place to start—as Julie Andrews sang in the Sound of Music. And the character of Maria in that musical, would be a good model for us. I propose some changes that could be costly. Before thinking that we cannot afford changes, keep in mind these two figures: People of the U.S annually spend $91,000,000, 000—that is 91 Billion Dollars—on gambling and 1,000,000,000,000,000—that is 1 Trillion Dollars—on Defense (Center for Defense Spending). I wonder if we are being wise with these expenditures when each figure is more than all of us in our country pay for food.

I hope you question this with me.

ON INFANTS AND TODDLERS

As mentioned earlier, we have our conscious beginnings *in utero*, so we need to take special care of the mothers-to-be. Let's start with free health care that provides positive education for the mother and her infant *in utero*, and later, for her, her infant and toddler. It is heartening to hear mothers say that they stopped smoking, drinking, or taking drugs when they are pregnant—and even better, when they continue abstaining after giving birth. Two of my sisters continued smoking and drinking alcohol when they were pregnant and, fortunately, had relatively healthy babies. I'm sure I could remove the "relatively" if the mothers had stopped both smoking and drinking. That was in the years between 1940 and 1960, and thankfully there has been a positive change since that time. Too many women live in such poor surroundings they have no idea how to treat themselves and their babies. I believe we can work together to remedy this.

Research in social psychology reveal that institutional change comes from outside the institution. The kingdoms of Europe and elsewhere did not decide one day that they should become democracies. It took years of writing and upheaval from outside the monarchies to bring about this revolution. Now those of us who yearn for a more truly free and enlightened spiritual life, are pushing religions institutions to accept all ethnic groups, gay marriages, birth control, women's right to choose giving birth, and more. Outside thinking, writing, and practices are pushing traditional churches to begin teaching a more lovingly spiritual God who is not micro-managing our lives and our world, and is not a being to fear, but is the force that empowers everyone and everything.

The "Divine Right of Kings, Czars, and Bishops," is gone. Now we must work to make sure that kings et al., is not replaced with CEO's and billionaires who control large corporations.

Next we need to have free day-care for all children and have it staffed by well-educated, well-paid and joyful staff members. The emphasis in these day-care facilities will be on play and self-acceptance, not on reading, math., and other academic subjects. Research shows that early emphasis on academics is counter-productive.

On Joyful Elementary And Middle Schools

I have heard rumblings that as more and more tasks are being done by machines, there will be millions of people unemployed. Where will they be able to find work? I believe that a large percentage of them are quite gifted in art, music, dance, drama, and athletics. Let's put them to work in schools. Every classroom could be a glee-club—not just have a glee-club, but BE one, with every student involved. And each class could be a dance troop, write and put on plays, participate in various sports, and enjoy every day in school. Everyone can sing—and off-key is good too, every child can dance, every child can act, and play on a team. Some schools currently are eliminating recess so they have more time to teach math and science. This is contrary to scientific studies and common sense; children do better in both areas if they are relaxed and begin their left-brain studies with a well-nurtured right brain. Each school day should have around two hours of play, creative activity such as dance, sports and singing. Teachers and schools who have experimented with this kind of program; scores will improve in math and science and other subjects when more time is spent in activities that relax and nurture the right-brains of students. Absenteeism and the drop-out rates decrease.

In my ideal school, no child will fear a teacher or coach. For too long we have confused respect with fear. In my first year as a priest, I taught religion to fifth, sixth, seventh, and eighth grade kids in the parochial school. I often walked around and watched the children at recess. The first and second graders would often crowd around me and I'd dance around with them and have a bit of fun. After a few weeks, two elderly women stopped me and told me that I should not let the children play with me like that, "Father, they will lose respect for you and the other priests."

I responded, "I believe they do respect me and I think you are confusing respect with fear. I do not want them to fear me or any other adult, unless that adult is mean or disrespectful toward them." The two ladies muttered derisive "Hummmphs," and walked away. I was rather proud of myself for having made the distinction between fear and respect; I had never thought of it before that morning. I've used it often since.

EMPLOY ALL SINGERS, DANCERS, AND ATHELETES IN THE LAND

In my dream school, we may have two or three children out of a hundred who will need medication for hyperactivity instead of around twenty now. We must stop trying to force the student into the school system and make the system a joyful place for all kids. So each grade would have three, four or even five teachers. Each classroom, or several classes in one house-like building, would have one "main" well-paid teacher and would be helped by the special teachers for that grade. A dance teacher would teach each first grade class in that school. If it is a small school, that teacher would teach all of the lower grades. The singing teacher would do the same.

In addition to having a specialty for that age group they would be joyful persons.

Every town and city is full of aspiring actors, dancers and singers who are waiting on tables or working at other menial jobs, hoping that some day they can realize their dream. Let's help them realize their dreams. Many young boys and girls love sports and dream of being professional athletes. They will jump at the chance to continue their passion by teaching. Some retired pro athletes are already doing just that. Put these talented people to work helping children enjoy movement and develop their own abilities. And there are thousands of other retired people who worked at jobs that were non-inspiring and would love to fulfill that dream of singing, dancing, play-writing, and all that.

I am sure that many people and educators will say that education should be work and not play. However, research indicates that children who are joyful and energized learn more and better. In one study, simply having fifteen minutes of mindfulness training and meditation lifted fourth and fifth grade students' mathematics scores fifteen percent. Both our daughters attended elementary and middle schools similar to what I have described and they both now have master's degrees and one works in an alternative charter school and the other is the editor of a university magazine.

There would be no A, B, C ... grades; the children would just be expected to complete certain learning tasks and when they were proficient in the area, they would move on to the next level. And there would be no standardized tests, so the teachers would be focusing on each child's learning and not on any tests. If the school or the district is interested in knowing if the children are learning, they would install video cameras in front of the class and periodically turn them on. If the children are learning it would show in their eyes. Children would cry when they had to stay home, not hate school and paint graffiti on its walls.

On Changing High School

For over twenty years now, I have been supervising interns at a community college in our Southern California area. There is no fence around the school and there is no graffiti. Our small city has three large high schools, each with around 3,000 students. The campuses each have a tall, prison-looking fence around it and still has a graffiti problem. At the college, the students choose the classes they wish to take and the time of the classes, when possible. No one demands that they attend a class and the teacher-professor can make his or her own demands on what attendance and how work gets graded. The students are free to come and go and to learn or to flunk out. In high schools, they are treated like they know very little and will go wild if they are given too much freedom. I'm sure you know this from experience. I would move to collegize the high school and treat the students as independent decision makers.

High school students would be given credit for tutoring in elementary, middle, and special help for the handicapped. There would be classes in woodworking, mechanics, engineering, plumbing, computer maintenance, all things electric, and other kind of skills that would help young people develop an interesting and job-related skills. Off-site credit would be offered for working accomplishments. College credit would be given for advanced academic work. Mean-spirited people need not apply as teachers or administrators.

Presently only a fraction of students of both sexes play any sports, except occasionally in gym class. I would have an extensive intramural sports program that every student could participate in—regardless of their athletic ability. Participation would replace gym class. At the end of a sport season, each school would have a tournament and the winners would compete with other similarly organized schools.

As you can see, the schools would eliminate our current spectator-driven student population and replace it with a participation-driven student body. I encourage you to wander around a large high school and just observe the students. You will see a very large percentage of students who are over-weight, stooped, and look sad and seem lost. We encourage this by the way we have organized our schools. Only the academically gifted or the very socially and athletically adept students seem to have a place—and many of them are insecure, too.

RESPECT AND CARE IN ALL TRAINING

I am sure that crime would decline in every town and city where this would be in operation. If we could expand this idea to the world— poverty and wars would decline and joy would abound. Yeah, I know, I'm sounding like a preacher. And that's OK, just so long as my teachings do not instill fear.

Sometime in the 1970's the Los Angeles Times had a feature article about an experimental training program involving the Los Angeles County Sheriff's recruits. The traditional training was similar to the military boot-camp model. Working with the University of Southern California and the University of California Los Angeles Sociology and Psychology Departments, the experiment went something like this: One hundred and forty recruits were randomly divided into the traditional boot-camp model and into a college campus-like more relaxed program. Participants in both programs were expected to become physically fit, extremely good at making choices and handling conflict, combat, shooting both rifles and pistols, and so forth. At the end the two groups were compared, and the "college-type" trained out-performed the harsher military-trained in every category. I have often thought of that program and wondered if the powers-that-be changed the training.

Treating people, from infancy through old age, with care and respect is always better than harshness, fear and all that goes with it.

If we instill a sense of joy and involvement in our educational institutions and media, instead of fear—as we now often do—we will find a much more productive and prosperous population. Historically, dictators arise out of fear-filled populations—not from peoples filled with joy and creativity. Perhaps a special tax could be laid on print, television, or social media that has an abundance of fear-inducing programs in its lineup.

So, in my thinking, if you want to live with yourself and enjoy it, you need to get the creative juices flowing, take inventory of your skills and interests and get off your duff. I'll leave you with this Christmas poem I wrote a few years ago—I don't think the song writer nor Louie "Satchmo" Armstrong will mind:

> *I see Christmas trees, menorahs, eid lanterns, and other signs too,*
> *Of people's faith in me and in you,*
> *And I think to myself, what a wonderful world.*
>
> *I see Christians, Muslims, Hindus, Buddhists and Jews,*
> *They work for peace and justice too.*
> *And I think to myself, what a wonderful world.*
>
> *The rules of many religions keep people apart*
> *And stop them from speaking from the heart,*
> *Still I see people helping people and smiling too.*
> *They're thinking and saying, "I love you."*
>
> *I see people hurting people and children shouting out,*
> *Stop, bring love, that's what it's all about,*
> *And I think to myself, what a wonderful world.*
> *Yes, I think to myself, what a wonderful world!*

THIS IS MY GRANDPA AND
HE IS TELLING US THAT WE
ARE CO-CREATORS OF OUR
WORLD, SO HE WANTS US
TO GET WITH IT.

ACKNOWLEDGEMENTS

Just as we cannot grow older or, even old as I have, and overcome our weaknesses, and heal our wounds by ourselves, a person cannot write a book by himself. First, I want to thank Anne, my wife of forty-five plus years, for putting up with me and giving up so much to marry me in the first place. Second to my daughters who have loved and supported me these many years.

I want to thank Thorn Sully, publisher, and artists and beautifiers, Niehl Zueleta for illustrations, and Teri Rider for cover and layout work. I want to thank my supportive writers' group, especially Russ Shor, Ed Coonce, and Patty Clark. Last but not least, I would like to thank Emily Corner and Kim Forgette for their time-consuming and helpful editorial work. Thank you all, without you, I would not have made it. And thank all of you, I sometimes think of my tribe, for supporting me in life itself. Because of you I would not have been able to live with myself and, at 83, even live. I hope I have been going with my heart always.

Don Hanley